1982

University of St. Francis
G   362.10425 B779

The Ethics of resource allocat...

W9-ADS-660

Edinburgh Medical Group

MORAL ISSUES IN HEALTH CARE

2

THE ETHICS OF
RESOURCE ALLOCATION
IN HEALTH CARE

edited by
KENNETH M. BOYD

EDINBURGH
at the University Press

LIBRARY
College of St. Francis
JOLIET, ILL.

© 1979
EDINBURGH UNIVERSITY PRESS
22 George Square, Edinburgh
ISBN 0 85224 368 5

Printed in Great Britain by
T. & A. Constable Ltd., Edinburgh

362.10425
B779

CONTENTS

103,422

Each of us finds lucidity only in those ideas which are in the same state of confusion as his own.

MARCEL PROUST

I pondered all these things, and how men fight and lose the battle, and the thing that they fought for comes about in spite of their defeat, and when it comes turns out not to be what they meant, and other men have to fight for what they meant under another name.

WILLIAM MORRIS

Preface

BECAUSE IT is the outcome of an unusual and original project, this is an unusual and original book.

With the expansion of medical technology, the accelerated increase in the cost of medical care and the growing expectation of expanded access to health care services, discussion in recent years has centred on efficiency and improved management. According to David Mechanic, there has been 'more than a noticeable lack of concern with medicine as a humane institution and with the motivations and ethics that govern its endeavours'. Yet ethical issues, both in the clinical sphere and in the broader sphere of resource allocation, are beginning to appear with increasing prominence on the health care agenda and we are no longer prepared to make the automatic assumption that value questions are exempt from, or not amenable to, that kind of rational discussion which is *de rigueur* in the sphere of 'hard science'.

Just as aesthetic awareness can be developed through communing with works of art, so, too, it is possible to develop a quality of ethical awareness which is just as important, in the decision-making process, as factual knowledge.

But with what, or with whom, do we commune in regard to ethical issues? Well, 'never mind the *system*, tell me about the *insights*' said Lord Justice Holmes in a famous letter to Harold Laski; and this injunction provides us with a clue as to how we can best develop ethical awareness. Factual knowledge may be best expressed in the objectivity of the text book, but there is no 'one best way' of acquiring ethical knowledge. In this field it is what Robert Redfield called 'the objectivity of the library' that matters, and there is no alternative to an approach which provides for the rich play, and interplay, of as wide a range of different perspectives as possible.

With these considerations in mind, in 1975, under the aegis of the Edinburgh Medical Group, a number of us, who belonged to different disciplines, agreed to come together, over a period of two years or so, to discuss the ethical aspects of resource allocation in the field of health care.

Even those members of our group who were accustomed to adopting a rational and highly-structured approach to their own special fields of work, accepted implicitly, if not explicitly, the peculiar appropriateness of the open-ended, group discussion type of approach to ethical issues which are, by their very nature, incapable of being resolved with any degree of finality as long as there is life on the planet.

In spite of this I think some of us may still, at the beginning of our project, have been more than a little uncertain about 'the open sea' and its infinite possibilities. I think it may still have been envisaged that there would be a stage in our discussions when we would be able to arrive at an agreed list of recommendations, or at a single, all-embracing formula, which would resolve the ethical problems of resource allocation, at least for the time being.

In fact, our task turned out to be a very different one. Since we were not directly confronted, in the context of our meetings, with real world problems in regard to which we had to take action, we inevitably found ourselves discussing the ethical problems of resource allocation in a more detached, but also in a more fundamental, way. In short, we discovered, in spite of ourselves, that we were less concerned to find solutions than to familiarise ourselves with the basic issues. What we were doing was learning how to think about ethical problems—because, just as there is a grammar of politics, so, too, there is a grammar of ethics.

At this point we began to realise that the real outcome of our project would not be solutions and remedies. Instead, we would have a new awareness of, and a new sensitivity to, the ethical aspects of health care systems, and a new insight into the kind of information that would help to resolve the ethical problems of resource allocation. We learned to accept the fact that the supreme value of our discussions would lie in the discussions themselves. Our meetings had no agenda in the ordinary sense, and our thought-processes were not so much linear as cyclical.

Similar considerations came into play when the question of our 'report' came up for decision. How could we submit a meaningful report on discussions which had issued from the void, and which, for the best of reasons, were due to return to the void? In the event, we asked the EMG Research Fellow, Dr Kenneth Boyd, to draft a series of papers on our meetings, which would be interpretive and elaborative, as well as reportorial, in character, and which would maintain the momentum of our deliberations by injecting into them a measure of objective feedback. Chapters 1 and 2 being introductory, descriptive and illustrative in character, chapters 3, 4 and 5 of this book are based on these papers, as they were revised during the closing stages of our project.

In setting our discussions within a number of frames of reference, Dr Boyd has been careful not to point the reader too firmly in this or that direction. True to the spirit of our enterprise he has concentrated on opening up the ethical issues of resource allocation in the field of health care, stressing, if anything, the difficulties, rather than the possibilities, that are inherent in the different approaches.

The papers in the Appendixes were presented to the group (which also had occasional inputs from visiting speakers) purely in order to stimulate discussion; and they are included here, not because the group has at any time endorsed them, but solely because they were part of what, in Scottish legal terminology, is called the '*res gestae*'.

The spirit of our times demands a 'hard-nosed' approach; but such an approach is by no means inconsistent with a resolute rejection of dogmatism, or of any attempt to over-simplify reality in accordance with a spurious scientism. How constricting, after all, to know the answers before the problems have been defined; and, even if it were not also a lack of integrity, how claustrophobic is the will to system!

The chapters which Dr Boyd has written, and the papers in the Appendixes, go well beyond what would ordinarily be called a report on our project and I hope that they succeed in conveying some impression of the extent to which a group drawn from a number of different disciplines developed a new awareness of the ethical aspects of priorities in health care, and experienced growth in human and personal terms, over a period of two years or thereabouts.

Historians used to pour contempt on the 'dark ages' of human history, when the human mind was presumed to have stopped functioning because there was no visible evidence that it was at work. Similarly there is always a certain hostility to groups which meet simply for discussion and debate. It is extremely doubtful, however, if the mind ever *does* cease to function; and, indeed, it may be at its most creative precisely when it is least productive in the ordinary, day-to-day sense. To those who have a nose for a book which records, however modestly, a genuine experience, and which is not just another collection of remedies, nostrums and *ex cathedra* pronouncements (however important these may be in a different context), this volume will constitute an absorbing attempt to make its readers think about the National Health Service in an entirely new light, and at a much more profound level than the 'management efficiency' one.

Preface

Quantity of health care has been our chief preoccupation since 1948; and there are some ways, it is alleged, in which the 1974 reorganisation has complicated this problem rather than simplified it; but it is an interesting fact that, since reorganisation, we have at last been talking seriously about quality of care, both in the clinical and in the organisational sense. This is a significant advance, and our project was surely a sign that, in the process of rationalising the administrative structure of the NHS, the 1974 reorganisation also introduced a strategic, or policy-planning, dimension into our thinking, and thus opened the way to new possibilities in the field of health care, and perhaps even to the possibility of a genuine synthesis between rational-efficient, technological imperatives and the demands of social justice and of humanity.

Our project, as I have said, was its own reward. That is true, but it is not true without a very important qualification, because it is my firm impression that our deliberations also had significant practical effects. In the first place, if we were able to clarify areas in which we differed, we were also able to mark out, in no uncertain manner, areas of consensus and positive agreement. Above all, however, in these days when *political* and *economic* rationality are all the rage, I am sure that our discussions had the long-term effect of depositing, at a deep level within each one of us, a residue, or 'sandbank', of *human* rationality, which was not there before, or which had been displaced, over the years, by more insistent pressures.

Written primarily, perhaps, *pour encourager les autres*, this book is the visible and lasting evidence of that very solid gain.

Drummond Hunter

13 September 1978

Introduction

THIS BOOK is based on the experience of a multiprofessional working group, convened as part of the Edinburgh Medical Group Research Project in Medical Ethics and Education. The working group was invited to consider ethical aspects of resource allocation in health care, identifying the moral issues involved, seeking consensus where possible and clarifying areas of disagreement. The method of study suggested and adopted was one of informed and sustained discussion among individuals with practical experience and practical goals.

The Edinburgh Medical Group was aware of growing educational, professional and public interest in moral issues in health care: it was anxious to promote wider discussion of resource allocation in this context; and it believed that a report from the working group could serve as a useful source book for other groups and individuals who wished to study the ethical issues. The present book was written with this end in view. Its contents, all of which derive from the working group's experience and studies, have thus been arranged to meet three broad aims: to identify some of the main moral issues; to provide information relevant to considering them; and to set them in historical and ethical perspective.

The book does this in two ways. Chapters 1 and 2, after introducing the problem and the method, describe, illustrate and comment upon a number of the group's discussions and its attempt to reach some conclusions. Chapters 3, 4 and 5, taking the form of a commentary on the issues, suggest some historical and contemporary moral perspectives, and a view of how to make the conflict between them more creative. These last three chapters are based on papers considered by the working group and revised in the light of its comments. Two further papers also considered by the group are included in the Appendix; the first is an introduction to the current debate in health economics, the

1

Introduction

second an empirical study of resource allocation in two health boards.

The working group on the ethics of resource allocation in health care was chaired by Mr T.D.Hunter (*Secretary, Scottish Health Service Planning Council*). Its members were: Professor A.D.Forrest (*Department of Psychiatry, University of Saskatoon; d.1979*), Dr W.M.Patterson (*General Practitioner, Edinburgh*), Professor J.S.Robson (*Department of Medicine, University of Edinburgh*), Dr H.Zealley (*Community Medicine Specialist, Lothian Health Board and Scottish Council for Post-Graduate Medical Education*), Miss N.Roper (*Nursing Officer, Scottish Home and Health Department*), Miss E.A.Shaw (*Senior Nursing Officer, Eastern General Hospital, Edinburgh*), Mr P.Bates (*Principal Officer, Child Care, Strathclyde Regional Council*), Mr R.A.H.Ironside (*Chartered Accountant, Edinburgh, and a member of the Lothian Health Board*), Mr A.M.D.Porter (*Lecturer, Department of General Practice, University of Edinburgh*) and Professor A.W.G.Manning (*Department of Zoology, University of Edinburgh*). The Secretary of the working group was the Revd. Dr K.M.Boyd (*Research Fellow, Edinburgh Medical Group*). The secretariat also included, as Medical Adviser, Dr C.T.Currie (*Lecturer, Department of Geriatric Medicine, University of Edinburgh*) and as Nursing Adviser, Dr A.J.Tierney (*Lecturer, Department of Nursing Studies, University of Edinburgh*).

ACKNOWLEDGMENTS

In setting up the working group the EMG Research Staff received helpful advice from a number of people. In particular, the staff wish to thank the Chairman of their Steering Committee, Sir Michael Swann, and its members, Mr T.D.Hunter, Professor R.H.Girdwood, The Revd. D.W.D.Shaw, Miss L.Hockey, Professor A.S.Duncan, Professor A.P.M.Forrest, Professor R.V.Short, Dr B.Potter, Dr I.E.Thompson, Dr G.Wright, Mr L.Gruer, Miss E.Scott and Mrs A.Wolf. The Research Staff are also grateful to Professor Sir John Crofton, whose advice on the composition of the working group was particularly valuable.

During its deliberations the group's thinking was stimulated by a number of guests, whose contribution it wishes to acknowledge, while in no way implicating them in this book's imperfections. These guests included Professor Rudolf Klein, Mr Robin Cook, MP, Mr Alex Fletcher, MP, Mr David Hamilton and Mr Skuli Johnsen. The working group is also grateful to Dr David Hunter, not only for making his research findings available to it, but also for agreeing to their publication in the Appendix to this

2

report. Dr Hunter is currently Research Officer to the Outer
Circle Policy Unit, London.

The Research Staff wish here also to thank the EMG Project
Office Secretaries, Mrs Margaret Cowell and Mrs Maureen
Bannatyne, whose patience, efficiency and cheerfulness were
indispensable factors in the production of this book.

The Chairman, Secretary and Members of the working group
are deeply grateful to the Trustees of the Leverhulme Trust and
the Nuffield Provincial Hospitals Trust for their generous grants
in support of the EMG Research Project. In this context also the
gratitude of the Edinburgh Medical Group as a whole must be
expressed for the contribution of the late Professor James Blackie,
without whose work and encouragement as Chairman of the
Consultative Council and Joint Grant Holder, the EMG Project
would not have come into existence.

CHAPTER 1

Problem and Method

THE PROBLEM of allocating scarce resources in health care raises some of the most difficult moral questions facing society today: but neither the nature of the problem, nor how society should tackle moral questions may be immediately obvious. This chapter therefore begins with a short statement of the problem, in terms of demand, supply and the options available. It then briefly illustrates the relevance of technical debate in ethics or moral philosophy to society's questions about the ethics of resource allocation; and it suggests that the technical debate has to be complemented by a method of multiprofessional moral enquiry. The rationale of this method is explained, with particular reference to the experience of the Edinburgh Medical Group; and the composition and general aim of its working group on the ethics of resource allocation are indicated.

THE PROBLEM

Demand. Advances in medicine and improved living standards have ensured that more people now live longer and healthier lives: but they have also heightened popular expectations of health and made continued medical progress a presupposition of public opinion. As a result, the amount of perceived ill-health in the community has if anything increased, while a more affluent society has bred maladies and injuries of its own. Coronary artery disease, some cancers, chronic bronchitis, road traffic accidents and certain aspects of mental illness seem, in one way or another, to be examples of this. In a more affluent society too, the ills of those who remain deprived may be more difficult to ignore; and the fact that all these developments have taken place in an increasingly egalitarian, democratic and informed society means that higher standards of care for everyone, as a basic right, are now not only expected but demanded.

Supply. Almost all of the resources needed to meet this demand are growing more expensive. With the receding threat, particu-

4

larly from infectious diseases, of death in infancy, childhood, and young adult life, the burden of health care has shifted towards treatment of acute illness, injury in middle life, and care of the chronically ill and elderly: but much of the first is increasingly costly in terms of investigative procedures, drugs and medical technology, and most of the last in terms of manpower. Cure and care alike, in other words, are taking more time and trouble: the expectations of more health service workers as well as more consumers are rising; and the budgetary implications are all too obvious. Despite escalating public and private expenditure on health care services, demand progressively outpaces supply. In Britain this became evident as the National Health Service approached the end of its third decade amid national economic difficulties: but the problem is not simply one of an immediate economic recession, and in one way or another it is endemic to the health care systems of all Western countries.

The options. When demand exceeds supply, in most spheres, there are generally five broad options to consider: increased expenditure, greater efficiency, voluntary restraint, rationing, and a policy of inactivity, masterly or otherwise. In the case of health care all of these options raise major difficulties; and these difficulties illustrate why moral questions are now so hard to avoid.

1) Increased expenditure, while still possible, is not a long-term option. The main reason for this is that while health service costs have been rising, so have those of most other items of public and private expenditure. Under these circumstances, no individual or nation is likely to be willing to foot health insurance bills which leave insufficient funds to pay for food, shelter, security, education and recreation, let alone to invest for the sake of future income. The moment of choice, perhaps, has not yet been reached: but with Western countries spending 6 per cent or more of a relatively-stationary gross national product on health services, and with the estimate, based on manpower trends during the 1960s 'that by the early 21st century half the population will be employed in hospitals',[1] it cannot be very far off.

2) Greater efficiency is possible in most spheres, and that of health care may be no exception: but while it is easy to produce anecdotal evidence of health service waste and inefficiency, it is more difficult to identify precisely where and how real savings can be made or efficiency improved. Unlike manufacturing industries, most service industries, and many bureaucratic operations, health care systems offer not only routine and restricted, but also individualised and somewhat open-ended services; and they do so moreover for symbolic as well as utilitarian reasons.

5

That 'everything that could be done was done' is not a criterion of effectiveness or efficiency, nor, for that matter, is the belief that poverty (and hence often multiple pathology) should be no bar to the best treatment. Which services are open-ended, when, where and how much, may seem rather arbitrary: but this reflects their establishment through an inevitably erratic history of perceived need, demand and opportunity, and their maintenance with an eye to largely unknown future, as well as present, needs. As a consequence, while greater efficiency may well be possible in some areas of the health service, in others it is difficult to determine exactly what constitutes greater efficiency; and overall there is no guarantee that greater savings and efficiency in one area will not lead to higher expenditure and less efficiency in others. What does seem certain however, is that such improvements in efficiency as are possible will not be achieved without an extensive process of negotiation among all concerned; and that value-judgments will play a crucial role in these negotiations.

3) Voluntary restraint, especially in the case of a growing demand, is very difficult to achieve. Often enough it takes either disillusionment with what is demanded, or some major crisis to bring this about: but a major crisis, in terms of the much-prophesied 'total breakdown' of health services is no more desirable than disillusionment with health—if that in fact is what people are demanding. Today, however, it is often suggested that what people are demanding is not health, or even health care, but health services; and those who suggest this often argue that the problem of supply and demand would be greatly alleviated if people took more responsibility for their own health, fitness and minor ailments. This argument unfortunately runs into difficulties, not only over the amount of health education resources required to promote effective self-care, but also over the very possibility of achieving it by such means—especially in a society where, it is argued, people are not given responsibility for many other life-determining decisions. Whatever the merits of this argument, what again seems clear is that if demand is to be reduced or even stabilised, it will first be necessary to achieve a measure of social consensus about the need for voluntary restraint.

4) Rationing, in the absence of increased expenditure, greater efficiency and voluntary restraint, may well seem the only option left. A great variety of rationing systems can be, and are, proposed today: some are based on demographic criteria, others on clinical, social or geographical; some, fairly crudely, on the ability to pay, others on enormously sophisticated questionnaire-based equations. Behind them all, however, lies the belief that some kind

6

of rationing cannot be avoided and must be implemented. While this may seem obvious enough to those brought up on the old ethics of thrift and restraint, or under wartime conditions, many other people, particularly those who have known only a relatively peaceful and prosperous, but also inflationary society will remain to be convinced of the need for rationing, especially when their own interests (or those of others they are concerned for) are at risk; and since practically any rationing system is unfair to someone, objections will not be difficult to find. In an older society such objections might have created fewer difficulties: hierarchy, authority and deference, or an obvious crisis such as war (as distinct from what seem the paper crises of economics) would have made the imposition of rationing easier. Today, by contrast, the case for it has to be argued.

5) A policy of masterly inactivity is probably the most difficult option to defend in public: in private however it may be the one most favoured by many politicians, administrators and professionals directly concerned with resource allocation. One reason for this, if what has been said above about the other options is generally correct, is the need for professional participation and public consent in implementing any measures designed to solve or alleviate the problem of supply and demand. To obtain participation and consent it may first be necessary for everyone to realise that their interests are threatened; and one way of provoking this may be by maintaining existing services as far as possible, while allowing events to take their course. This, it can be argued, will probably result in a general lowering of standards, sufficiently gradual to avoid 'total breakdown', but sufficiently perceptible to encourage professionals to become more cost-conscious and the public to lower their demands or accept rationing. While hoping to achieve this, the protagonists of masterly inactivity will also be aware that the history of medicine is full of unexpected triumphs and disasters, and that of politics, of forgotten unsolved major crises. In the light of these, it is always possible that active policies of political accommodation to currently perceived problems will run the risk of being too successful, in that they may render medicine and society less capable of meeting unforeseen challenges. At present, perhaps, there is little danger that resource allocation policies will be too successful: masterly inactivity however, at least has the advantage of keeping the options open until the conditions necessary for any interim solutions can be created.

Masterly inactivity, on the other hand, is not without its risks: those who employ it are always in danger of being replaced by others who promise (however unjustifiably) more active and

B   7

energetic solutions; and there is also the risk that falling standards will provoke, not responsible participation and consent, but deeper sectional conflicts with even worse consequences. This is particularly likely if masterly inactivity is interpreted as a political device of divide-and-rule (which it may well be); and consequently professionals and the public may find, in the policy's means, an excuse for not helping to achieve its ends. The reality of these risks today thus militates against such a policy and certainly against anyone admitting to operating it. It is difficult to escape the conclusion however that its ends remain the right ones.

This brief outline of the problem suggests then that material, educational and democratic progress has created major obstacles of participation and consent, which stand in the way of any proposed solution. These obstacles, at the same time, suggest the possibility of greater political maturity. Under these circumstances, Government clearly has a responsibility to inform professionals and the public, as straightforwardly as possible, of the facts and options. Professionals and the public however also have a responsibility, not simply to offer objections, but to indicate how far they wish to see which options exercised; and to give reasons for their choice. Since the choice is fundamentally a moral one, and since many of the reasons for it will be based on value-judgments, a responsible answer from the professions and the public will thus have to be based, to some degree, on examination of the ethical questions involved.

METHODS OF MORAL ENQUIRY

In an educated and democratic society then, it can be argued, the professions and the public have a responsibility to examine the ethical questions raised by the problem of resource allocation in health care. The danger with statements of this kind, however, is that they may remain a matter of political rhetoric, unless viable methods of moral enquiry can be found. It is not enough today, in other words, simply for individuals and groups with common interests to make value-judgments or moral assertions (of the kind found, for example, in pressure-group pamphlets, political manifestos or the idiosyncratic memoirs of retired surgeons), for while often illuminating, such contributions are, equally often, mutually contradictory. Something more critical is needed therefore, a method of moral enquiry which seeks reasons and justifications for these moral assertions and value-judgments, and which is able to compare and contrast them in the hope of reaching some measure of public consensus.

Moral philosophy. Perhaps the most obvious method of this

kind is that of the academic discipline of Ethics, or Moral Philosophy. In that discipline moreover there is nothing new about studying the ethics of resource allocation. Moral philosophers have had an interest in the subject of distributive justice for centuries, and there are numerous philosophical theories about it. Some of these theories argue that people should be treated equally, others according to what they deserve, and others again according to what they need: some have been based on the will of God or the natural order, others on calculating the effect on the common good, and others again on the general will of society. Such theories have been constructed, criticised, refined and justified by countless moral philosophers, often at considerable length, but rarely to the satisfaction of all of their colleagues. Their obvious inability to reach any final agreed conclusion about justice however is not simply the result of perversity on the philosophers' part. Anyone who takes the trouble to formulate his own commonsense views about justice into a theory, and then tries to justify that theory to someone with an eye for consistency, coherence and correspondence with reality, will soon find himself in the same labyrinth. The fact is that justice, like other important ethical concepts, is a highly complex idea, whose complexity reflects that of the human mind, human society and the human environment. It is not surprising therefore, after centuries of discussing these complexities, that philosophical arguments have often become very technical, and to some extent difficult for the layman to follow.

The technical nature of philosophical discussion does not mean however that it need be inaccessible to laymen who are prepared to learn its language; nor does it mean that moral philosophy is unrelated to everyday life or without influence upon it. Two relevant examples which illustrate this are 19th-century Utilitarianism and the Theory of Justice propounded by the contemporary American philosopher John Rawls.

1) Utilitarianism, the theory that the good of a rule or action is to be tested by its usefulness, particularly in terms of human happiness, is a fairly clear example of the influence of a set of philosophical ideas on everyday moral judgments. Since its appearance in the 18th century, Utilitarianism has been widely reflected in popular attitudes, and arguments based on Utilitarian principles have carried considerable authority. (So much so in fact, that in a recent discussion of ethical questions a medical student was heard to remark that 'we should get back to the Biblical fundamentals, such as doing what is for the greatest good of the greatest number'.) Its influence in the resource allocation context can be seen, for example, when a case is being made

for choosing one or other of the different options mentioned in the previous section of this chapter: the case, repeatedly, is made in Utilitarian terms of achieving some balance of benefits over disadvantages.

A major problem with arguments of this kind however, as was suggested earlier, is that of persuading others of their validity; and this problem has its counterpart in terms of ethical theory. Thus although Utilitarian philosophers have made considerable efforts to refine their doctrine, it remains highly vulnerable to criticism. On the one hand, no one is sufficiently omniscient (or sufficiently sensitive to the different things different people want and need) to make the long-term universal calculations it requires. On the other hand, many people are prepared to argue that utility is not in any case the only criterion of a rule or action's good: an eternal moral law, or people's intentions, or the general will are all, it may be argued, equally if not more important criteria. Dissatisfaction with Utilitarianism on these and other grounds thus leaves the field open for other theories, at the philosophical level, about the moral bases of social action; and the wide interest recently shown outside philosophical circles in Rawls' theory, is perhaps some indication that the question is of more than academic interest.

2) Rawls' Theory of Justice may well have attracted so much attention because it seems at first sight to hold out the possibility of providing a philosophical framework within which the competing claims of justice and freedom might be reconciled; and hence some working consensus ultimately achieved, in a free society, on goals and priorities. Rawls' approach is to ask what a group of ordinary men and women, rational and acting in their own interests, would choose as principles of justice, if they had to make a binding choice in temporary ignorance of their own abilities, psychology, conception of the good and status in society. In this hypothetical situation, he argues, the general conception chosen would be that 'all social values—liberty and opportunity, income and wealth, and the bases of self-respect are to be distributed equally unless an unequal distribution of any, or all of these values is to everyone's advantage'. [2] More specifically, Rawls states, the 'principle of the greatest equal liberty' ('each person is to have an equal right to the most extensive total system of equal basic liberties compatible with a similar system of liberty for all' [3]) would be given priority over what he calls the 'difference principle' ('social and economic inequalities are to be arranged so that they are . . . to the greatest benefit of the least advantaged' [4]). This priority is defended on the grounds that those choosing

10

would not be willing to sacrifice the certainty of retaining their basic liberties to the less than certain hope of regaining them once social and economic inequalities had eventually been ironed out.

This last point makes it understandable why Rawls' theory has been criticised as a somewhat circular justification of Western democracy against Communism, taking the values of the former too much for granted and not taking seriously the latter's criticism of them. Rawls himself argues that his principles are compatible with a socialist and even a feudal system, as well as a democratic one; and he goes to considerable lengths to defend his argument from many other criticisms which might be made of it. The result is a highly refined and impressive theory, in the Social Contract tradition, which offers an alternative to Utilitarianism in an age sceptical about Natural Law theories. As such it retains a great deal of plausibility. The fact that many other philosophers nevertheless continue to criticise it, and that many of their criticisms also sound plausible, tends however to dampen the hopes of the wider audience seeking a philosophical framework for social consensus. Their hopes are dampened too by the difficulty of working from Rawls' second order principles, based on a disputable hypothetical situation, to the more immediate problems of contemporary social goals and moral priorities.

These criticisms and difficulties do not mean however that the basic intuitive ideas behind Rawls' theory are not going to be influential, or that his work may not contribute eventually to viable practical solutions of the resource allocation problem. Philosophical criticism of Utilitarianism, after all, did not prevent it from being enormously influential, or at least from having a remarkable elective affinity with the culture in which it was produced. The point here however, and the reason for introducing the examples of Utilitarianism and Rawls, is to show that philosophical debate of this kind today is normally conducted at several removes from the scene of resource allocation, and that the connection between it and the day-to-day dilemmas of health care is somewhat tenuous (as non-philosophically-inclined health workers who have read the previous few paragraphs may appreciate). The implication nevertheless is not that such philosophical discussion is irrelevant, any more than laboratory research is irrelevant to patient care: it is, rather, that it needs to be complemented by other methods of moral enquiry, somewhat closer to the scene of action.

Before turning to these other methods, one further point about moral philosophy should perhaps be added, although to some it

11

will no doubt be a statement of the obvious. It may be thought, since philosophers have toiled so hard and so long over the genuine complexities of ethical questions, that those who lack knowledge of the philosophical arguments are thereby less capable of weighing up and answering the questions involved in moral issues. This, in fact, recently seems to have been implied by an eminent contemporary philosopher, when he asked,

how would you solve practical problems unless you knew which were good and which were bad arguments, and how would you know *that* if you did not understand what the questions meant? [5]

In reply to this however another no less eminent philosopher made the point that knowing what a question means is not the same thing as being able to formulate it in technical philosophical terms; and it was simply a matter of fact, he said, that

many people who have never bothered their heads with philosophers' perennial disputes as to the meanings of questions about what ought to be done are, nevertheless, very good at reaching answers to such questions, even in very delicate and complicated cases. [6]

Multiprofessional moral enquiry. What seems to be needed then, is a critical method of examining the moral questions of resource allocation, which steers a middle course between the heat of political debate and the disinterested study of moral theory. The working group on whose experience this book is based represents an attempt to employ the method of interdisciplinary and multiprofessional group study to this end. This method is neither particularly original nor particularly complicated; and given time, enthusiasm and limited back-up facilities, it is not difficult to reproduce. It may be helpful therefore, first to explain its local background and general rationale, and then (in the next chapter) to describe how it operated.

1) The local background can be explained briefly. The Edinburgh Medical Group had been established in 1967, to provide an independent and non-partisan forum for the interdisciplinary and multiprofessional study and discussion of moral issues raised by the practice of medicine. Like the London Medical Group before it (and Medical Groups in most other British medical schools subsequently), it had been set up largely on student initiative; and its programme of lectures, symposia and conferences on relevant social and moral topics met an evident need, not only among students, but also among practitioners. In time however, many of those who participated came to believe that it would

also be helpful if some of these topics could be examined in greater depth than was normally possible in the Edinburgh Medical Group programme.

This request, in other words, was for some kind of research activity to complement and stimulate the growing educational role of the Edinburgh Medical Group. It was not immediately apparent however what kind of research was appropriate in this context, since conventional models, including the academic study of moral theory and the various social scientific options, were probably employed to the best effect in their respective disciplinary contexts. It was therefore only after extensive discussion, in Edinburgh and with the other Medical Groups, that the possibility of an appropriate form of research became apparent. This, it was agreed, would have to reflect the Edinburgh Medical Group's interdisciplinary and multiprofessional interests, its involvement of informed lay opinion in its discussions, its concern with medical and nursing education, and above all its basic motivation as a body specifically concerned with moral issues in health care.

With these considerations in mind, the Edinburgh Medical Group and the University of Edinburgh proceeded in 1975 to set up a research project in medical ethics and education. The project is funded by the Leverhulme Trust Fund and the Nuffield Provincial Hospitals Trust, and it has a small research staff, made up of two research fellows (a philosopher and a theologian) and four part-time research advisers (a geriatrician, an obstetrician, a psychiatrist and a nurse). It has the general aim of developing methods of study and research in medical ethics, partly through curricular and extra-curricular study programmes, and partly through multiprofessional working groups investigating particular moral issues in health care. The latter include the working group with which this book is concerned.

2) The general rationale of the multiprofessional working group method can also be briefly stated. It is, as has already been pointed out, a traditional and reasonably straightforward way of investigating moral issues. It also, in fact, returns to the methods which the founding fathers of moral philosophy suggested for that discipline, and particularly to the methods of Socrates and Aristotle. Socrates' method was to ask critical questions of experts and to engage in rational debate, in the hope of establishing a public consensus about the issues and how to decide them: he also showed, albeit with the help of Plato's dramatic imagination, how to develop the full potential of the symposium as a method of moral inquiry. Aristotle, rather more specifically, argued that

13

ethics should begin, not from abstract principles, but from the actual moral judgments of people with some experience of life. Its task, he believed, was to seek, not mathematical precision (which was not in the nature of its subject matter), but general clarification of the issues in the interest of reaching some broad consensus for practical purposes.[7]

The method adopted by the Edinburgh Medical Group followed these general guidelines. The working group on the ethics of resource allocation was made up of fourteen members, from different backgrounds and disciplines, who were invited to take part after preliminary discussions which suggested that their personal as well as professional viewpoints represented a broad cross-section of opinion. The members included four doctors (a psychiatrist, a physician, a general practitioner and a community medicine specialist), two nurses, with experience of research and administration as well as practice, a social worker, an accountant who was also a health board member, an economist and a zoologist: its chairman was a health service administrator, and its secretariat comprised one of the research fellows together with a medical and a nursing adviser. The professional members were all familiar, on a day-to-day basis, with a wide range of resource allocation problems, while the lay members all had some knowledge of health care.

The working group was thus able to begin its task from the familiar ground of its own knowledge of, moral views on, and value-judgments about the subject. From these beginnings, it was hoped, the working group might move on to clarify some of the moral issues, establish areas of consensus and disagreement, and provide, through personal and professional contact as well as publication, some stimulus and also some resources for wider discussion of the issues. The aim, in other words, was to engage in the kind of critical and co-operative moral enquiry which might help to create the conditions for resolution, in practice, of the current dilemmas of resource allocation in health care. In the next chapter a brief account will be given of that moral enquiry, and the conclusions it reached.

REFERENCES

1. Cooper, M.H. (1975) *Rationing Health Care*, p. 36. London: Croom Helm.
2. Rawls, J. (1973) *A Theory of Justice*, Chapter II, 11, p. 62. London: Oxford University Press.
3. *op. cit.* Chapter V, 46, p. 302.
4. *ibid.*

5. *The Listener*, 13 April 1978, p. 473 (letter from Professor J. Wisdom).
6. *ibid.*
7. Aristotle, *Nichomachean Ethics* Book I, Chapters 1–3. Harmondsworth: Penguin Classics 1955. *Vide* Thompson, I. E. 'The implications of medical ethics', *Journal of Medical Ethics*, 1976, 2.74–82.

CHAPTER 2

Records of a Group Experiment

THE LAST CHAPTER began with a short statement of the problem of resource allocation, and further perspectives will be outlined in Chapters 3 and 4. But getting moral problems into perspective is easier in retrospect than in prospect, particularly in a multi-disciplinary context. This chapter is about how the working group attempted this task. It begins with a general description of how the group got under way, of the main stages of discussion, and of its concluding tasks. It then records the course which discussion took during three of the stages, concerned with different levels of resource allocation and with the different points of view of those involved in the process. Some particular discussions are also recorded in greater detail. Finally, the group's attempt to reach conclusions is described and commented on.

GENERAL DESCRIPTION

Initial questions. In setting up the working group, the Edinburgh Medical Group had been anxious to avoid predetermining the course of its discussions by imposing any prior categories or pre-suppositions. It was up to the working group itself, in other words, to decide both what the relevant issues were and, within the general guidelines mentioned in the last chapter, how it would discuss them. In order to get the discussion started, however, the research staff had prepared a list of questions which the working group was invited to respond to at its initial meeting. These questions, while not intended to be exhaustive, were designed to raise a wide range of ethical issues, in terms of basic principles, the rights and responsibilities of health care users and providers, and the circumstances of decision making. The list was as follows.

A) *Principles and rules*
   1. What moral and political principles should inform decisions about: (a) the deployment of money and manpower within the National Health Service; and (b) the selection, other than on

clinical grounds, of individuals for intensive and other scarce forms of care?

2. What considerations of justice, equality or fairness should be involved in these decisions? And how should these be weighed against considerations of social consequences, utility and the common good?

3. Is it possible today to devise general moral rules about the allocation of scarce resources in health care? If so, how absolute should such rules be? Or how far should they be flexible and altered by cases? If it is not possible to devise such rules, by what is decision-making to be guided?

B) *Rights and values*

1. Does every individual have an equal right to life and health? Can the value of the life of one individual be weighed against that of another?

2. On what grounds are the rights of an individual and the value of his life determined? Can rational discussion of these grounds uncover common ground? Is it either possible or desirable to create a synthesis of what the major religious, political and other world views teach about these rights and values?

3. In the selection of patients for intensive and other forms of care, how should clinical factors be weighed against non-clinical? In particular, should account be taken, and if so how much, of non-clinical factors such as socio-economic status, sex, employment prospects and family responsibilities, and partly-clinical factors such as age and psychiatric background?

C) *Moral agents*

1. Who (politicians, economists, administrators, professionals, patients, government, the public in general) has the right or the responsibility to be involved in making decisions about the allocation of resources?

2. What relative weight should be given to the claims of individual conscience, of professional ethos, of government and of public opinion? What are the limits of individual responsibility, clinical freedom, government and public control?

3. What are the moral implications for decision-makers of having to think in terms of the comparative rights and value of individuals or sections of society?

4. How far should identification and sympathy with individuals or sections of society influence decisions, and how far should emotional disengagement and the attempt to be objective or scientific?

D) *Circumstances*

1. What are the moral implications of making decisions about resource allocation through (a) the market system, or (b) collective planning by rational-scientific or step-by-step methods?

2. What are the moral implications of the need to make decisions in crisis situations (i.e. economic or clinical crises)? Are longer term checking and balancing procedures required? If so, of what kind?

3. What account should be taken of what might be called 'the moral drift of history', as it affects changes either in public opinion or in professional ethos? How far are moral rules, or rules of thumb, about resource allocation the product of social or cultural factors no longer operative or relevant? Does this affect their ethical status?

4. What account should be taken of the limits of human freedom, the contingency of human existence and the possibility of an irreducible tragic element in life? What is scarcity?

The working group agreed to discuss these questions at its first session, and they proved a useful device for eliciting its members' initial moral views and value-judgments. In retrospect, it seems clear that the questions did not predetermine what the group was to perceive as the most significant issues; nor did the questions provide, at the time, any immediately satisfactory way of focussing the problem.

Areas of disagreement and agreement. What the questions did reveal were a number of significant areas of disagreement within the working group. It was soon apparent, for example, that opinion was divided on the part played by self-interest in determining priorities. Some non-medical members, responding to the first set of questions, suggested that the principles governing resource allocation were influenced, all-too-often, by self-interest, and in particular by the economic interests of professional staff. A better basis, they believed, would be provided by making social equality and the common good the goals of resource allocation; and to achieve this, they argued, greater administrative and political control was necessary.

This view was not shared by all of the professional participants however; and some medical members of the group argued strongly that in so far as self-interest was a significant factor, the self-interest of professionals was more evident in the search for excellence than in the desire for economic advantage. They also argued, in response to the second set of questions, that while in principle all individuals had an equal right to life and health, in

18

practice inequalities would always exist. Because of this, bureaucratic control, motivated by the mirage of equality, could only act as a brake on progress: but the interests of professionals, channelled and controlled by their peers, coincided with those of the public and individual patients, if not now, then certainly in the future. Professional self-interest, seen in terms of the quest for excellence, thus not only served the common good, but also reflected the general will.

Disagreement of this kind did not mean, at this stage or later, that the group was to split between the professionals and the others: opinion on both sides of the professional fence was too diverse for this, and the discussion of practical problems was to raise too many qualifications. Even at this early stage, responding to the third set of questions, the professional members of the group were far from unanimous about, for example, the desirability of consensus decision-making, or indeed about whether it was ever possible to be truly rational in determining health care priorities. Nor, in discussing the fourth set of questions, did they reach agreement about some practical matters which were raised, such as the inadvisability of taking health policy decisions in isolation from decisions about the social services, housing and education.

Two points of agreement did emerge. The first, arrived at reluctantly, was that the working group should try to confine its study to British, or at most, Western health care. The moral issues raised by resource allocation in and to the Third World were without doubt highly significant: but the Western world seemed, for better or worse, a social laboratory in which the problems of progress were being explored, and the National Health Service, for all its faults, was still a significant experiment of the middle way. If the group was to be concerned with moral issues, therefore, it had a responsibility to examine them in the environment which it knew best, rather than in one about which information was limited, and for the most part second-hand.

The second point of agreement was reached with regret rather than reluctance. It was that current methods of resource allocation were haphazard, random and pragmatic: that this was attributable to pressures, individual influence, emotional factors and political involvement; and that what seemed to be missing today was an agreed frame of reference, within which resource allocation decisions could be made and different health needs weighed up one against another.

Procedure adopted. No such agreed frame of reference was apparent from the working group's initial exploration of the

19

subject: and although some members could probably have provided one, which some others might have agreed to, the group as a whole was not prepared at this stage to pre-empt its discussion by polarizing it around any particular theoretical frameworks. Its preferred procedure, which was reached partly by conscious decision and partly by trial and error, was to accumulate a variety of practical and theoretical perspectives on resource allocation in a wide range of health service contexts. This procedure, it was believed, at least would yield insights, at most the beginnings of a framework. The members of the working group, in other words, were to be rather like primitive cartographers, exploring territory which, while often familiar, afforded no very high vantage points; and occasionally encountering, as they extended their explorations outward in different directions, a number of other mapmakers, whose claim to have been up in a balloon they doubted.

This procedure involved the group, during the first eighteen months of its existence, in an extended programme of private study and group discussion. Its exploration of the issues moved from concrete examples to theoretical constructs and back again to concrete examples. In practice, although this was not always clear at the time, there were *five* main stages of discussion during this period. The *first* examined resource allocation at, respectively, day-to-day level in a particular area of health care (that of mental disorder), health board level, and national level. The *second* was concerned with how professional staff, administrators and users of health services saw some of the problems involved: and it also examined some theories about the relationship between these groups. The *third* stage repeated the pattern of the first, beginning with a particular area (that of primary care) and moving on to health board and national levels, although not in quite the same way as before. The *fourth* reviewed and criticised current work in health economics and manpower planning. The *fifth* returned to topics discussed during the third stage, and considered empirical data about health boards and theories about politics.

A more detailed account of the first three stages will be given in the next section. These stages are interesting to record because they show the working group moving towards a greater appreciation of the complexity of its subject matter, and of the problem's intractability, at least as far as practical solutions were concerned. The remaining two stages were no less valuable to the group's understanding of the problem: but by this point the discussion was taking an increasingly shorthand form, and the new material introduced at these stages can best be illustrated by the papers in the Appendix (on which much of it was based) and by some of the excerpts of discussion.

These five stages, then, represent the working group's exploration of its field. Through this process some of the moral questions became clearer, and sometimes the possibility of some agreed answers seemed in sight: but as a consequence of the critical-consensus method of study and the nature of the subject, the focus of discussion frequently slipped and, as further implications were explored, the answers tended to slip away. By the end of the eighteen months, however, the members of the group were thoroughly familiar with the literature and the issues, which they had also discussed with several guests, invited because of their special knowledge of particular topics. A number of members, moreover, had participated in Edinburgh Medical Group student seminars and conferences on the subject, as well as innumerable informal discussions outside the group, but provoked by it. With this experience behind it, the last six months of the working group's existence were occupied in two tasks. The first was to consider a series of papers, prepared by the group's research fellow in the form of an interpretative commentary on the issues: these papers, revised in the light of the working group's comments, appear below as chapters 3, 4 and 5. The second, and more difficult task was to produce some agreed statement of priorities in health care. The attempt to do this is discussed later in this chapter.

THREE STAGES OF DISCUSSION
The first three stages of discussion can be described most conveniently here by taking the first and third together, before turning to the second. The first and third stages, as already indicated, each followed roughly the same pattern, beginning with a particular area of health care, and then going on to health board and national levels.

Mental disorder. The particular area chosen on the first occasion was mental disorder, and it was readily agreed that this unglamorous field seemed unjustifiably deprived of resources. Did this mean that basic health care needs were not being met? And were there inequalities here which should and could be remedied?

In reply to the first of these questions, a nurse with some experience of this area argued that certain basic health care needs were not being met. Hospitals for the mentally disordered, she observed, were unattractive to nursing staff, particularly because of the high degree of incontinence among patients. In addition, recent visits by the advisory service to long-stay wards in one Scottish health board area had revealed the highest incidence of extensive and deep pressure sores seen by the visitors in over ten years. The acquisition of pressure sores by patients in shorter-stay wards, she noted, had provided successful grounds for damages against health boards elsewhere. Yet wards of from twenty-eight to fifty mentally disordered patients, some of them incontinent, were still left in the care of only two nurses overnight, during which time each of the nurses had to leave the ward twice for meals. In terms of overall statistics, the picture was no less stark. Although 45 per cent of NHS beds were for the mentally disordered, only 21 per cent of nurses worked with these patients and only 11 per cent of consultants were psychiatrists: only 14 per cent of NHS expenditure was spent on hospital and community services for the mentally disordered; and only 9 per cent of the Medical Research Council's budget was invested in this area. Even the food served in these hospitals, another member added, was cheaper.

To the nurse, these examples suggested that basic health care needs were not being met. 'The achievement of continence, and the deposition of urine and faeces in a socially accepted receptacle, and in private,' she argued, 'makes human beings different from other animals.' But this aspect of human dignity was being disregarded by default in many long-stay wards. Society meanwhile took little notice of the inequalities involved, for staff as well as patients, until the staff's human reaction to their environment produced the occasional highly-publicised incident involving cruelty to patients. When this happened the nurses were punished. But were the resource allocators blameless? And was the administrative conscience salved, in the case of pressure sores, by paying damages?

Basic needs were not being met, and it certainly seemed that the inequalities involved ought to be remedied. But how? The obvious answer was to provide more resources, including manpower, in the hope that this would improve both morale and care. Since it seemed unlikely that the total NHS budget would be increased, the only way of providing these resources was by gradually increasing expenditure on mental disorder at the expense of what currently were more glamorous and prosperous areas, such as intensive care and neurosurgical units, where heroic efforts were often made to keep patients alive. There might even be, the nurse added, a certain dreadful wisdom in doing this, since in addition to the twilight survival of some patients saved from death by neurosurgery, there was growing evidence of psychiatric disturbance in other post-intensive therapy patients; and the large resources currently allocated to these areas might already be contributing to the future demand for long-stay wards.

Other members of the group agreed that more resources should be allocated to mental disorder. But some remarked that resources allocated to hitherto deprived areas were not always fairly or wisely distributed within these areas, especially if they had to be used to the limit for the limit to be maintained. It was also pointed out that redistribution at the expense of currently glamorous areas might be a false economy. The crucial capital investment in these areas had already been made: reducing the proportion spent on maintaining them, far from making them more efficient or effective, might mean underutilisation of expensive equipment, demoralisation of the staff involved and scientific stagnation. If reallocation were to be beneficial, the process had to be a gradual one, and the case for each new investment carefully argued on its specific merits.

Such necessary qualifications, the group agreed, made it difficult to generalise about basic health-care needs or remediable inequalities. Specific examples from mental disorder had been given, and broadly agreed to. But when someone suggested that the group attempt to draw up a list of basic health-care needs, it felt itself being drawn into rhetorical generalities, producing an agreed baseline which was too low for most members' individual satisfaction or for most patients' practical advantage. An agreed list of remediable inequalities had similar drawbacks, compounded by the fact that much information about inequalities was not available. But even if it were, the group felt, the uses to which it might be put were limited. The comparison of inequalities seemed, essentially, the comparison of dissimilar unquantifiables, and thus more a matter of value-judgment than any basis for reproducible, information-based decision making.

In agreeing to more resources for mental disorder then, the group felt that it was making a gesture of human solidarity rather than advocating a rational policy with measurable beneficial results. It also felt that its sentiments were in line with a growing trend in public opinion on the subject, which might well influence health policy. Noting this, one or two members of the group expressed anxiety that this trend might divert resources from what, they believed, was the more urgent need for *prevention* of mental disorder, specifically in terms of ante-natal diagnosis and therapeutic abortion. Gestures of human solidarity with mentally disordered individuals now alive were no doubt appropriate: but in making these gestures it was important not to be sentimental about the quality of life and the quantity of suffering involved.

No amount of resource allocation to care could more than mini-
mally improve or alleviate that; and where cure was impossible,
prevention should be much more actively promoted, despite
many people's scruples on the subject of abortion.

The group as a whole, while agreeing that prevention was
desirable, doubted the political wisdom of an over-active prevention policy, insensitive to scruples. The scruples mentioned raised
genuine moral difficulties for many parents and professionals, and
had to be taken seriously as ethical factors in resource allocation.
But if the group disagreed on this, its discussion of mental disorder had produced two major points of agreement: 'basic health
care needs' was a relative notion, which had more to do with social
bonding and society's self-respect than with any objectively
measurable criteria; and the comparison of inequalities, being the
comparison of dissimilar unquantifiables, provided no practical
basis for decision making. These were points of agreement to
which the group was to return repeatedly, by different routes, in
many subsequent discussions.

Primary care. The second area chosen was primary care, and on
this occasion the group was concerned with more practical
questions about the use of time and the division of labour. Time,
a general practitioner pointed out, was his scarcest resource.
With the development of group practice, appointments systems
and laboratory facilities, the pattern of work had changed: but in
a practice with, for example, four doctors and eight thousand
patients, the work-load of each general practitioner had in fact
increased. Allowing for holidays and sick leave, the average
doctor's working time per week could be fifty-seven hours, plus
thirty-four hours on call, and the number of night calls was much
greater than in a single-handed practice. Group practice moreover
did not mean that patients no longer wished to see their own
doctor at consulting times; and for the conscientious doctor, pre-
ferring a comprehensive consultation to a series of short inter-
views, the average length of each consultation was nearer ten
than five minutes. A further minute or two, unimportant at the
time but cumulatively significant, could be added if the practice
had decided, for example, to record the blood pressure of all
consulting patients, as a routine measure to identify asymptomatic hypertensives. And then in order to make such decisions,
to exchange information and to act as a critical peer-group,
practice meetings also were required, the time taken by these
being increased if the work of district nurses and health visitors
were to be properly integrated with that of the doctors.

24

Listening to this account of the time resource in general practice, some members of the group asked if there was no way of 'unloading the trivial' parts of the doctor's workload. Nurses, one suggested, might be consulted more often in the first instance and decisions about further treatment subsequently made in consultation with the doctor. The general practitioner agreed that this could be done, but perhaps not a great deal more than it already was: many patients would feel inadequately done by if they did not see a doctor, preferably their own one; and good whole-person and personal care required close collaboration between the doctor and nurse, which, while beneficial, might not be time-saving. There was also the possibility, a nurse added, that 'unloading the trivial' might become what it suspiciously sounded like, in other words that nurses might find themselves performing routine and repetitive technical tasks, which doctors found uncongenial. Where this had happened, some nurses had initially welcomed the prospect of taking over medical responsibilities, but had eventually found this unsatisfying. Nursing had its own distinctive and discretionary contribution to make to patient care.

It did not seem then as if changes in the doctor-nurse division of labour were likely to increase the time resource in general practice. This led one lay member to ask if the group was perhaps being insufficiently radical in its thinking on the subject. Was there not a danger, he asked, that overtrained doctors were pricing themselves out of a market in which basic skills would suffice? In many countries, family planning services, for example, were run by paramedical personnel, who gave pills and injections and performed early abortions: in South Korea contraceptive pills could be bought in a supermarket, in New York one hospital was run entirely by nurses, doctors being called in only when necessary, and even in some British family planning clinics patients were assessed in the first instance by nurses. No doubt there were dangers in this, but there were also dangers in taking an aspirin or other forms of self-medication, and these were readily accepted by most people.

The view that general practitioners might be overtrained for many of their tasks received support from some other members of the group, who asked if primary care might not be better provided by an intermediate grade of practitioner? Examples of this were the Chinese barefoot doctors, the Russian feldshers, paramedical personnel in the British armed services and a similar grade being trained by some American medical schools for work among civilians. In response to this suggestion, other members of

25

10 3, 422

College of St. Francis Library
Joliet, Illinois

the group objected that none of these examples really corresponded to the needs of primary care in Britain. In the USA general practice was relatively weak; in the armed services the needs were those of a young and basically healthy population; and in Asia and Africa, social, cultural and health conditions created very different expectations of medical care. In Britain, by contrast, general practice had retained a significant role in society and its services were among most people's basic expectations. To replace this structure, and those of community nursing and health visiting, evidence was needed not only that any new system would be more effective and efficient, but also that it would be equally acceptable. At present this seemed unlikely.

This argument did not satisfy all members of the group. Returning to the example of Chinese medicine, some suggested that the problems of resource allocation in British general practice were due, in part, to the fact that the NHS was basically an ill-health service, and that the average general practitioner, with two thousand patients on his list, was in no position to provide anything else. In China, by contrast, people were organised into populations of about six hundred, which was an ideal unit size: everyone could know everyone else, and on this scale health education and health monitoring were a real possibility, with individuals feeling responsible for their own health and for community health care provision. This, it was agreed, was an attractive possibility. But how far did such arrangements depend on political coercion or the Chinese tradition of collective behaviour? The group as a whole was sceptical about the possibility of such a revolution in attitudes and expectations taking place in Britain.

Within the limits of British politics and psychology, the group did agree that some changes in the primary care division of labour were possible. It accepted, after further discussion, that nurses and health visitors might play a larger part in first consultations, particularly in family planning. This idea, it thought, ought to be explored on the grounds of effectiveness rather than economy. The group also discussed the role of receptionists and their responsibilities. Some of its discussion was rather anecdotal, and one doctor observed: 'patients are polite to the doctor, rude to his wife, and very rude to his receptionist. Why?' Several members of the group replied that while many receptionists were highly competent and courteous, some were not, possibly being over-zealous protectors of the doctor's time. Part of the reason for the anecdotal nature of its discussion of this subject, the group reflected, was the lack of research on the training and practice of receptionists. Such research, it believed, might be profitably undertaken by health authorities.

Health board decisions. The working group's exploration of health board decision-making (of which several members had experience) took the form of two simulation exercises, devised by Dr Helen Zealley. In the first, members were asked to argue the case for and against proposed savings and new projects, as well as existing policies and projects. In advance of the meeting they were provided with a series of briefing sheets, on which they could also make their own suggestions and calculations.

The briefing sheets were prefaced by an introductory paper which explained the role of the Treasury, the Scottish Home and Health Department, and health boards in the process of resource allocation. The Treasury allocated total sums of money between different Ministers and Departments: by and large, this procedure had been dependent on repeating the previous year's allocation, plus a standard arbitrary percentage for new developments. The Scottish Home and Health Department allocated money and scarce manpower between different area health boards: recent allocation of development funds had attempted to introduce a distribution of resources based on health service needs. Health boards considered detailed requests and demands, and were the major allocators of funds for defined purposes. At each stage in this complex multiphase process, consideration had to be given to many factors, including decisions made by other groups which had a direct effect upon the details under discussion.

The significance of external decisions on the use of health board funds was then illustrated by Table A, which listed national decisions influencing allocation, their estimated cost, the consequences of expenditure, and constraints to development. The national decisions included a variety of salary increases and additional contractual and training commitments which involved an inevitable additional revenue expenditure, for the annual budget under discussion, of £4,910,000. The total budget for the year under consideration was £50,000,000, while that for the previous year had been £44,000,000. Thus without savings elsewhere, most of the increase in allocation was already committed by these national decisions.

In addition to these salary commitments there were several other national policy decisions to be taken into account. These included promises to develop preventive and community-based services and to implement equal opportunities legislation: but, for the former, new money was unlikely to be available, and no child care facilities were to be provided for the latter. National policy also required health boards to seek advice from professional advisory committees and from local health councils: but in practice these were likely to give conflicting advice. The health board nevertheless was expected to take all these policies into consideration when allocating the £45,090,000 which remained.

The health board also had to take into account its own existing expenditure and policy commitments, which were listed on Table B. This estimated that £43,500,000 (revenue) and £500,000 (capital) was required in order to maintain existing services. Since 75 per cent of this would be spent on the remuneration of individuals covered by employment protection legislation, most of this sum was pre-committed. If all of it was spent, the amount remaining for allocation was £1,090,000.

The health board's current policy commitments were to develop services for the elderly and the long-term handicapped. In terms of specific new projects, a geriatric assessment unit was almost completed and a 30-bed long-stay unit for the elderly was already built: the full-year revenue cost of these two projects was £235,000, thus reducing the amount available to £855,000. Other specific health board projects, and their estimated cost were:

	REVENUE	CAPITAL
a new theatre complex, to reduce waiting lists	£150,000	separate budget
day hospital services for eighty patients	£100,000	
expansion of renal dialysis services	£28,000	
a nursery for children of female staff	£10,000	£50,000

The total expenditure on these projects, if proceeded with, would thus amount to £338,000 of the £855,000 available.

Table B also had a column for proposed savings. It suggested, for example, that changing the use of a small acute hospital might save £100,000 per annum. But it pointed out that a change of this kind would certainly be resisted by the hospital's staff, and the community or clientele it served (examples of this might be local or women's hospitals), and that this resistance would probably receive government support. The table then left spaces for other savings to be suggested by working group members.

Members' suggestions about new projects and possible savings varied considerably, but about half of the group suggested abandoning the new theatre complex (mainly because they doubted whether it would in fact reduce waiting lists) and supported a change in use of the small acute hospital (although some pointed out that the sum involved was trivial). Abandonment of the nursery, the day hospital and the renal service expansion, in each case received some support from two or three members. Further savings, each suggested by some of the members, included rationalisation or reduction of maternity beds, reduction in acute beds, and not recruiting, or reducing, the number of administrative and medical staff. In the light of constraints (particularly on the last suggestion), the need for negotiation, and consequent delays in implementation, these savings were difficult to cost however, and estimates varied.

By this stage the health board was left with between £517,000 and £955,000 to allocate. Table C illustrated its options by listing recommendations from within the board and from other bodies about how this should be done. Proposals from within the board, and their estimated cost, included:

	REVENUE	CAPITAL
replacement of broken major equipment		£350,000
five-year pilot study for an intensive local anti-smoking campaign	£50,000	
expansion, by one patient per week, of coronary by-pass surgery	£12,000	
replacement of coronary care ambulance	£5,000	£5,000
introduction of genetic register and counselling service	£8,000	
routine serological screening for spina bifida prevention	£30,000	£80,000
expansion of contraceptive services	£25,000	
fluoride programme for caries prevention	£60,000	£200,000
improvement of catering management services	£30,000	
improvement of dental anaesthetic service	£25,000	

The total expenditure on all these projects, if proceeded with, would thus amount to £880,000. Proposals from other bodies, however, also had to be considered, and these included: a recommendation from the Hospital Advisory Service that lavatories be improved at a long-stay hospital which might be replaced in five years—capital cost £20,000; a refusal by the Higher Medical Training Committee to give accreditation to a training programme without additional medical staff—revenue cost £10,000, capital unknown, but extra accommodation might be needed; and a request from the Social Work Group for the NHS to provide home helps for the elderly—revenue cost £100,000. The total cost of these recommendations from other bodies was thus at least £130,000, which added to the internal recommendations amounted to £1,010,000. The sum available, as already mentioned, was between £517,000 and £955,000.

Confronted with these figures, members of the working group concentrated, not surprisingly, on what could be cut back or resisted. Considering the recommendations from other bodies, members sympathised with the aims of the Advisory Service and the Social Work Group, but doubted whether the health board could or should take responsibility for the means, at least at present. Of the internal recommendations, the anti-smoking campaign and contraceptive services received the least support, while the fluoride programme and dental anaesthetic service received most. It had been pointed out, in Table C, that significant benefits to the NHS from expanded contraceptive services and the fluoride programme would not be apparent for many years: but members seemed more prepared to back these than the spina bifida screening and the genetic register, to which the same considerations applied.

Members were asked, prior to the meeting, to estimate the total cost of the savings they would make and the recommendations they would support, in order to produce a balanced budget. Most members found this extremely difficult, and felt that their own proposals were somewhat arbitrary. At their meeting, which initially took the form of a mock health board meeting, they found it no less difficult to reach agreed conclusions. There was some agreement on what ought to have lower priority, a list including acute and maternity services, health education and administration: but general principles were difficult to establish, and members were acutely conscious of how little they knew about the hidden implications of any decisions they might take, and of the constraints on implementing these. One member eventually remarked that the working group was simply a group of people sitting round a table discussing matters of which they were far too ignorant. Members who had served on them, immediately replied that this was a fairly accurate description of what health board meetings often felt like.

Conscious of this problem, the working group went on to ask more radical questions about health board decision-making. There was some support in the group, for example, for a more radical approach to staffing levels. In some areas of the health service, it was generally agreed, these were too high: but no agreement could be reached on how to reduce them; selective redundancy, it was thought, would be opposed by trade unions, while natural wastage, although perhaps of necessity the only method practicable, created a dysfunctional staff profile. An alternative radical approach to cutting costs, it was suggested, was by not offering treatments of unproven effectiveness, and alcoholism and parasuicide treatment, as well as intensive coronary care were offered as instances: but such services, it was pointed out, were already established, and any withdrawal, without totally convincing proof that they served no useful purpose, would be opposed by those who provided them, by client groups and by public opinion. A third suggestion was that decisions should be made more information-based, by instituting more operational research on the total health budget: but this, it was pointed out, would entail heavy additional research costs, and decision-making could well be impeded by information overload.

There was one point, however, on which all members of the group agreed. This was that the introduction of fees for an item of service (particularly in relation to family planning), while still a relatively small budgetary item, represented an unwanted and dangerous innovation. A further point, which was also of some interest at the time (early in 1976) concerned the freezing of salaries over £8500. Some members of the group argued that this enabled highly paid professionals to set an example for the general good. Others pointed out that, since the measure was arbitrary and enforced from above, it was likely to have little moral effect, while it had certainly lowered morale among those affected: nor did it have any significant effect on the health care budget.

The working group's second simulation exercise, six months later, took the form of a meeting asked to plan major changes, over a period of ten years, in the hypothetical health board's services. Its objectives, in line with Government recommendations of the time were:

1) to increase the provision of nursing and other caring facilities for the elderly;
2) to improve facilities for the mentally and physically handicapped;
3) to rationalise the provision of acute services;
4) to explore techniques for reducing the demand and need for services.

Briefing papers for the meeting made the following observations about the resources available to meet these objectives:

31

a) *Buildings*: the existing buildings in which health service activities occur are unlikely to fall down for at least fifty years;

b) *Equipment*: major promotion drives to sell sophisticated supplies, equipment and drugs will be mounted by manu-facturers whose work force is at risk from unemployment;

c) *Manpower*: more nurses with a basic training are available to work than at any time in the past. After an initial increase in emigration rates for three years, doctors are expected to demand major changes to their career structure in view of the increasing numbers of British graduates;

d) *Money*: it is assumed that there will be: (i) no change in the total revenue resources available to health boards, and that inflation will continue to reduce the value of this sum to below its present value: i.e. less real revenue money will be available; (ii) no money will be available for major capital developments; (iii) only small sums will be available for specific capital projects; (iv) all health service workers are likely to expect considerably higher salaries from the fixed sum available, as soon as wage restraint is removed.

The briefing papers also suggested a series of specific proposals for meeting the objectives. To meet the first, for example, ten small hospitals could be developed as community nursing homes: the revenue cost of this was estimated at about £500,000. This, it was suggested, could be set against £1,000,000 saved by first withdrawing in-patient and major diagnostic services from these hospitals, while the remaining £500,000 saved would cover the cost of centralising the acute services in three specialist hospitals, in order to meet the third objective also. A further £50,000 saved by ensuring optimal use of sophisticated diagnostic equipment could be set against £50,000 to be spent on improving living conditions for patients in long-stay handicap hospitals (second objective); while £80,000 saved by reducing the number of junior medical staff in the small hospitals could be set against £80,000 to be spent on expanding the number of general practitioners to meet increased commitments. A policy which encouraged ambu-lant long-stay patients to share normal domestic responsibilities, such as cleaning, minor repairs and redecoration, could save up to £50,000 in domestic and maintenance costs. This sum could be set against £20,000 to appoint a voluntary help co-ordinator to each community nursing home, and most of the £25,000 needed to establish a small multiprofessional health board 'think tank' charged with finding ways of introducing new disease-prevention measures, improving existing services, reducing duplication in the provision for services and reducing demand for services. Other proposals, mostly about integrating hospital and community services in terms of medical and nursing manpower, would involve no change in expenditure, if the other proposals were implemented.

At the meeting to consider the health board's ten-year plan there was, initially, considerable approval of the specific proposals, as a rational approach to the problems. But members of the working group had each been asked to represent particular professional, administrative, trade union and community interests; and in this capacity they raised numerous objections, about the change in use of the small hospitals, the manpower-use implications for all grades of staff, the use of voluntary help and other aspects of the proposals. Their grounds for objecting will be obvious in the light of comments in other sections of this chapter. Conscious of the political nature of many of these objections, but often personally in favour of the proposals, members of the working group believed that while a ten-year plan of this kind was desirable, detailed studies of the cost and effectiveness of the specific proposals were necessary for them to succeed. To this end, the group was not prepared (on financial grounds) to invest in a health board think-tank, and, as already mentioned, it was suspicious of large studies which took too long and were too general to be of much use. It did believe, however, that limited studies of specific options were both politically useful and politically necessary, if proposals of the kind under review were to be implemented. But some members were pessimistic about the possibility of rational long-term planning: the health service, they believed, had been too long accustomed to respond to government policy and public opinion with 'panic-flap management'. A further major hindrance to rational planning, at least in the Scottish context, was the lack of co-ordination between health and the social services.

National policies. The general objectives under consideration at the second health board simulation exercise had been conceived in the light of the Scottish Home and Health Department's 1976 memorandum, *The Way Ahead.*[1] This was one of several policy documents which the group had examined in some detail. The others included the parallel DHSS consultative document *Priorities for Health and Personal Social Services in England* (1976),[2] the further DHSS consultative document, *Prevention and Health: Everybody's Business* (1976)[3] and the Government public expenditure white paper of the same year.[4] They also included two

33

independent publications of a more radical nature, but representing different viewpoints: the Unit for the Study of Health Policy's *Health, Money and the National Health Service* [5] (1976) and the Office of Health Economics' *The Health Care Dilemma* (1975). [6] Members of the group made extensive comments and criticisms of each of these documents, but we shall concentrate here simply on the last two and on the Scottish memorandum.

The Scottish memorandum, like its English equivalent, had been framed within the economic limitations of the 1976 public expenditure white paper. The former Secretary of State for Scotland, in his foreword, explained that this called 'for restrictions on public expenditure . . . at least until 1979–80' in order to have 'resources available for investments and exports and to get back on the path to economic growth'. [7] The government, however, was allowing continued health service growth, although at a lower level than in earlier years. Describing recent trends in the health service, the memorandum noted that proportionately more of the considerable real increase in expenditure had gone to hospital as opposed to primary and community care and that within the hospital sector, acute and maternity services had particularly benefited. It also noted that despite improvements in the utilisation of facilities, it remained 'a paradox of the present system that so much is spent on ineffective cure while so little is done to encourage the public in general to improve its own health'. [8]

Turning to recommendations on finance and the deployment of services, the memorandum suggested a slowing down in the building programme and an emphasis on facilities for geriatrics and mental disorder. In terms of revenue expenditure it indicated that improvements in high priority sectors depended on savings elsewhere, and it underlined the importance of rationalising services, particularly in the hospital sector. As immediate priorities, the memorandum listed the following:

1) Promotion of health care in the community through the progressive improvement of primary care services and community health services;
2) More positive development of health services for families in areas of multiple deprivation;
3) Lessening the growth rate of the acute sector of the hospital service;
4) Continued improvements in hospital and community health services for the elderly, the mentally ill, the mentally handicapped and the physically handicapped;
5) Encouragement of preventive measures and the develop-

ment of a fully responsible attitude to health on the part of the individual and the community. [9]

The immediate response of most working group members to this memorandum was one of general approval. It was a 'fair attempt' at planning, commended for its 'epidemiological realism': but a variety of conflicting qualifications were also offered. On the subject of maternity services, some suggested that a greater cut-back was needed, while others argued that any cut-back involved the serious danger of an increased incidence of brain damage and mental handicap. Increased emphasis on family planning was both commended—for its effect on breaking the cycle of deprivation; and criticised—as an expensive way of medicalising a social problem at a time when the birth-rate was already falling: one member suggested that it would be more effective to limit family allowances to first and second children only. Improved services for the elderly were thought necessary, but it was argued that the resources should go to 'comfort services' rather than technological medical services, which some saw as a form of 'medical undertaking'.

On the transfer of greater resources to care of the mentally handicapped, there was general approval, although some argued that greater demedicalising of mental illness could lead to savings, and one member remarked, on mental handicap: 'I shrink from euthanasia, but cannot help thinking about it: we appear to accept it for severe cases of physical handicap, for example spina bifida, and perhaps we would accept it for thalidomide children, were they to be born today'.

The proposal to improve primary care and community health services also received qualified support. Several members argued that reduction in the length of hospital stay would require greater resources than envisaged, for health visiting, community nursing and social services; and the need for joint planning with the latter was again stressed. Blanket social service expenditure was criticised however, with special reference to unemployment benefit, and low cost solutions using voluntary groups were commended. Several members warned that a shift in emphasis to general practitioner and primary care would not necessarily be more economical, especially if the amount, for example, of screening was increased. Demedicalisation was again raised here, one member suggesting that an appropriate counselling service could decrease the general practitioner's workload, while others argued for greater restriction of the general practitioner's drug account.

The memorandum's attitude to growth in the acute hospital

sector was received sympathetically, but the economic implications were questioned and it was pointed out that the 'increasing sophistication and therefore cost of medical treatment' affected only a very few patients. It was also argued that excessive standardisation of patient stay could lead to further depersonalisation of hospitals. As far as self-care, disease-prevention and health education were concerned, most members considered the memorandum's intentions admirable, but also vague; and in the light of current Government revenue from cigarette and alcohol taxation, somewhat ambivalent. In order to increase efficiency, members recommended, variously, greater and less control of clinical freedom, programme budgeting, medical audit, and 'a brisk weeding of drunks, dements and other incompetents' in the NHS.

The group turned next to *Health, Money and the National Health Service*, published by the Unit for the Study of Health Policy. This had been selected as an example of left-wing analysis. It began from the assumption that NHS priorities could not be divorced from broader economic considerations, and questioned whether the UK's poor economic performance would be improved by cutting back public expenditure, a strategy which made recovery of economic health dependent on a decline in the population's health. A major flaw in this 'orthodox' strategy, it argued, was the pursuit of indiscriminate rather than purposive and selective economic growth. The latter, it suggested, could be promoted in ways which did not produce the pattern of injuries and illness which much contemporary health service activity was engaged in ameliorating. It was necessary, therefore, 'to give greater emphasis to the promotion of well-being through increased attention to the role of the socio-economic environment in the "production" of ill-health; through the fostering of confidence in people's outlook on health matters, and through a greater emphasis on more humane and more ecological approaches to health service delivery'.[10] This, it argued, implied a shift in the focus of health policy 'from questions concerned simply with the level and distribution of services towards questions of public information and education, towards less expensive and less technologically elaborate services and towards socio-economic policies that affect health'.[11] Britain, it suggested, might be in a unique historical position as a pioneer of 'the transition into post-industrialisation —that is, into a stage of socio-economic development when people and resources mattered'.[12]

Members of the working group were asked if they agreed with this document's criticism of economic 'orthodoxy' and with the health goals it recommended. In reply, a third expressed agreement, but some of these members found it difficult to see how the desired changes could be brought about. Others thought that the document's economic arguments were not fully substantiated, and considered its proposals 'economically naive'—unless complete control of life styles on a communist basis was envisaged. The majority were sure that 'a new approach to society's goals, economic and otherwise, was vital for survival': but some saw this in terms of a greater willingness 'to give a full day's work for a full day's pay, which would produce better productivity, less boredom, and a greater pride in achievement: this in turn would lead to a feeling of well-being and a desire to keep fit and well'. The document's health goals, by contrast, were less controversial, at least in principle: members believed that there was 'evidence that in geriatrics and paediatrics, for example, cheap prevention might delay, or eliminate the need for, expensive intervention'.

The Health Care Dilemma or 'Am I Kranken, Doctor?' published by the Office of Health Economics, was chosen as an example of right-wing analysis. It began by examining the nature of ill-health in terms of interaction between the challenge of a specific disease and the state of the individual challenged, noting the multifactorial causation of disease and the influence of social and psychological factors on the process of becoming ill. Diagnosis by a doctor, it pointed out, might 'confer' a disease on the patient, adversely affecting prognosis and legitimating sick behaviour; while over-enthusiasm about 'the clinical iceberg' could lead to over-diagnosis with no real benefit. The problem was further complicated by the medicalisation of social problems, which turned the doctor into a pastor (for which he was not trained), reduced the general practitioner's medical role (offloading it on to the hospital) and introduced the dangers of 'healthocracy'. The underlying problem was that the 'shift from pathological investigation to (highly expensive) diagnosis at the molecular level'[13] had occurred when public expectations of what doctors could do were unrealistically high. A more realistic definition of health was needed. Ill-health should 'be seen as a failure to respond and cope satisfactorily with the normal periodic challenges which every human being must face in his lifetime'.[14] Both the public and the professions should be less willing to see ill-health in terms of factors over which the individual has no control: the medical profession should be less willing to legitimate such behaviour. To this end self-care was needed. Doctors should tell the public that failure to achieve the WHO state of perfect well-being was normal, but that invalidism represented failure. Health education had a part to play in this; and, for doctors, a proper appreciation of psychological, social and environmental factors. The concept of normality had to be demythologised; and the notion that the discovery of a new disease represented a medical success had to be discouraged. Given measures of this kind, the publication concluded, 'it is possible that many of the existing "shortages" under the National Health Service could be eliminated without the employment of additional resources'.[15]

Members of the working group expressed qualified agreement with this document also. It illustrated, one member suggested, the 'inevitable match' between 'Illich and Enlightened Toryism' and was 'perhaps to be applauded for its tendency to lower inappropriate expectations generated by post-1948 assumptions of total welfare'. But its goals, several members pointed out, were like those of the previous document; admirable in principle, but difficult to implement except in the very long term. 'In the short term' one member remarked, 'until our population in Britain can get down to twenty-five million or so, I foresee things getting worse'; and another pointed out that doctors would find it very difficult to avoid legitimising sick behaviour as long as the National Insurance system remained, in effect, 'a scheme for having doctors rubber-stamp statements of symptomotology put forward by patients'. A few members, however, were less sympathetic to the document's goals: one thought it 'punitive', while another considered that 'the model outlined and subsequent solutions are gross over-simplifications of complex problems': there was no evidence that a 19th-century self-help approach worked.

Taking together these three documents and the others mentioned, the working group had found much to commend as well as to criticise. In further discussion, it agreed that the problem of health care priorities was less a matter of what was desirable than of how it could be achieved. Waste and inefficiency in the National Health Service should be weeded out: demographic challenges should be met; the aged, the handicapped and the chronically ill should receive effective care in comfortable surroundings, and in the community where possible; a wealthy society should also be a healthy society; self-care and realistic expectations of health should be encouraged; professional and public education should be geared to these ends. All this, however, required the political will and the political means, and because of this, the group believed, change would be slow. Members of the health professions, it acknowledged, had a clear responsibility to take political initiatives in this process: but at present there was some truth in one member's suggestion that the health professional was still, and not totally unwillingly, 'like the chaplain to a pirate ship'.

National politics. The political role of health professionals was discussed again by the working group, when it met with some backbench Members of Parliament and others with political interests. The aim of the meeting was to explore how desirable changes, of the kind discussed by the group, might be brought about politically. In response, the Members of Parliament observed that Parliament was not the primary decision-making centre in matters of health policy, and that even what it did decide was not greatly influenced by backbenchers. What they were able to do, through lobbying, depended very much on the pressures brought on them by the public: but very little such pressure was brought in health policy matters, and their contribution was also limited by the average Member's lack of information on the subject. For the most part, Members heard either from professionals about too much administration and about union problems, or from individuals about personal issues: in relation to the latter at least the Member was often able to be effective, by taking the matter up with the health board, the Department, or the Minister.

One aspect of this account, questioned by the group, concerned the possibility of successful lobbying. A number of local examples were discussed, and some complaints were made about the 'unhelpful and secretive' reaction of civil servants to requests for the kind of information required by potential lobbyists. The Members of Parliament agreed that this was sometimes the case, but they pointed out that an appropriate remedy existed through Members at Westminster, who could ask for the required information. In their view, just as many difficulties were placed in the way of reform by the indecision of professional advisers on health matters. Ministers were often criticised by the health professions for making 'political' decisions about health policy or for giving in to vocal pressure groups: but one important reason why they did so was because the health professions failed to present a united front on the subject. The Members of Parliament believed that if the health professions, or even the medical profession alone, could reach some agreement about what they considered desirable health policies within the economic constraints obtaining, then civil servants and politicians would find it very difficult to resist their advice.

Before the second health board exercise and the meeting with Members of Parliament, the working group had spent some time, in the second stage of its discussion, attempting to see the problem of resource allocation from the point of view of some of those most intimately affected by it: professional staff, administrators and patients. The rationale of this discussion was fairly obvious: while 'do as you would be done by' might be a laudable moral maxim, others sometimes wish to be done by differently; and those engaged in moral enquiry should, if nothing else, attempt to understand the reasons why.

1) *The professional perspective.* Clearly no single perspective could represent the point of view of all professional staff, and the group asked first how an average hospital doctor was likely to experience the problem. The immediate answer, based on several members' experience, was that he would probably be rather overwhelmed by its growing scale and complexity, and that faced with rising public expectations, he might feel some nostalgia for the simpler problems of the past. The crux of his problem, it was suggested, was society's failure to recognise the limits of hospital medicine; and one doctor put it like this: 'medicine doesn't cure people; it patches them up. For example, many people think you go to an acute medical or surgical ward to be cured. This is not true; if you get "cured" you probably did not need to go there in the first place. Medical treatments are basically "illness amelioration treatments" and many surgical treatments remove one problem, for example a peptic ulcer, but produce others in its place.'

Was this how the average hospital doctor saw his work? Privately he might admit as much, but in public many were less willing to do so, perhaps believing that the mythology of medical effectiveness had its therapeutic uses. The mythology nevertheless was at the root of the problem; it had grown up around the real although limited clinical skills and effectiveness of medicine, but under its penumbra large areas of life had become medicalised, sometimes with little justification. Care of the old and the mentally handicapped, for example, had been medicalised, in part at least, because medicine seemed to offer a technique for discharging humanitarian impulses which society felt, but was not prepared to accept responsibility for. But although society might feel that old people 'were better cared for' in long-stay wards, in fact the medical contribution to their welfare was limited. The specific contribution of medicine here was primarily a matter of assessment, and for the great majority of old people, community support was more desirable than hospital care. In this area, as in that of mental handicap, the goal was to maximise the use of the individual's own assets, and to give life an element of human dignity. This was largely an educational task, in and of the community, and medicine's role in it was specific and limited. It was certainly not a matter of creating more long-stay wards.

The creation of long-stay wards, however, was precisely the kind of investment which the mythology of medical effectiveness tended to encourage, and in subscribing uncritically to that mythology, hospital doctors in the past had helped to create some of the problems of scale and complexity which their successors now faced. These problems arose partly because government tended to allocate resources in fits and starts, so that they were often irrationally distributed within the hospital sector, but once distributed difficult if not impossible to redistribute. Illustrating this difficulty from the area of mental handicap, a member of the group described how additional domestic staff had been employed to clean wards during a period of relative national affluence, when it had also seemed possible (and therapeutically desirable) for patients to be employed in sheltered contexts outside the hospital. When economic conditions grew worse, the patients had to return and other ways of employing their time found; but the domestics remained. And, or so this member alleged, 'the wards are less clean now, with expensive cleaners, than they used to be when the patients cleaned them'.

The feeling that things were simpler in the past, and resource allocation easier, was shared by other medical members of the group; and it was agreed that nostalgia for simpler problems probably made many hospital doctors impatient of contemporary ones. The irritants were often petty enough things, such as the inconveniences caused by the centralisation of tea-making or laundry facilities: but cumulatively they created frustration, and from time to time a sense of angry impotence, as when industrial action at a distant laundry prevented all but emergency admissions. Confronted with such situations many hospital doctors remembered times when local difficulties could be solved more personally: when, for example, the hospital secretary would disappear down a manhole to discuss his drains, and his grievances, with the hospital plumber; and remembering this, some had begun to adopt the philosophy that 'small is beautiful' and to ask whether the National Health Service existed to provide care or to provide jobs. It was too early to say, perhaps, whether this combination of nostalgia and frustration would lead hospital doctors to what might be considered a more realistic view of the hospital's role: emphasis on community rather than hospital care, after all, might lead hospitals to lose limbs rather than fat. The outcome ultimately depended, not only on the medical profession's willingness to be honest 'about what can be cured and what must simply be borne', but also on its ability to communicate this to individual patients and the public at large.

41

This then was how some hospital doctors in the working group saw the point of view of their average colleague; and their advocacy of community care and 'small is beautiful' was endorsed by lay and nursing members, although the latter expressed some reservations. More nurses, like more patients, they believed, ought to be moved out into the community: but establishments were still highly inflexible, and until nurse education was reorganised on a more generalist basis, too few nurses had the necessary experience. In the meantime, while the role of nursing might well be extended, it was a mistake to see that primarily in terms of the nurse taking on delegated medical functions, as a way of saving doctors' time.

Reservations about moving patients out into the community were also expressed on behalf of general practitioners. General practitioners might not encounter quite the same kind of problems as hospital doctors, but many found it no less difficult to allocate their limited resources, and not least their time. During recent decades the workload in many practices had increased considerably: a family doctor was likely to see over 98 per cent of his patients over sixty-five at least once annually and many of these, of course, more often. He also had the responsibility of making a correct decision for forty or fifty patients a day. It was understandable therefore that many general practitioners were apprehensive about any shift in emphasis from hospital to community care. Aware that it was almost impossible to reduce manpower levels in the public service, and knowing that hospitals represented nearly three-quarters and general practice less than a tenth of NHS expenditure, they suspected that proportionately fewer resources than patients would move into their area. They agreed, certainly, that 'small is beautiful': but not if this philosophy was applied to the hospital at the expense of general practice.

2) *The administrative perspective.* Turning to the administrative perspective, the working group asked in particular how nurse administrators viewed the problem of resource allocation. Their point of view was considered of particular interest, partly because nursing accounted for about half of the hospital service's salary bill, and partly because nurses were professionals with intimate experience of patient care, who had recently been given a much greater say in controlling their own affairs and planning their own future.

The nurse administrators' main preoccupation, as represented to the working group, was securing the means to maintain an acceptable standard of patient care; and although they viewed this as a difficult task, they did not consider it entirely impossible.

The difficulties related both to money and to manpower, the latter being less serious than the former. Interestingly, in the light of earlier discussion, it was suggested that long-stay geriatric wards were one area in particular need of greater investment; the need, however, was not so much for more of these wards as for upgrading the facilities for existing geriatric patients, whom it was unrealistic to expect now to return to the community. Improved facilities, with some separation of day and sleeping areas, were also necessary if nursing staff were to be attracted to working with geriatric patients.

Acute areas were generally better staffed and nursing morale there was on the whole higher: in this connection the nurse administrator was more likely to be concerned with the lack of supporting social work services and the problems created for her colleagues in community nursing by earlier discharge of patients. Earlier discharge added a great deal of interest to community nursing, and for this it was welcomed: but, as for general practitioners, it meant a heavier work load, and this was not matched by an increase in staff, since community nursing was held to a very strict establishment level. Hospital nursing establishments of course were also tightly controlled; but in hospitals this was offset to some extent by the replacing, through natural wastage, of untrained by trained staff.

The point of view of some nurse administrators thus did not seem overly pessimistic, at least as far as resource allocation in the hospital sector was concerned. But it was argued that this point of view was perhaps more common in the better sort of small hospital; and the working group was warned that standards of patient care were only maintained by the greatest vigilance, and the risk of falling standards was very real. As it was, one nurse commented, economies had been made to the limit, and the loss of what administrators might consider the trimmings (continental instead of full breakfasts for patients, for example) might seem like falling standards to patients, who were not aware of the effort involved in maintaining clinical priorities. A further problem which troubled some nurse administrators was that of maintaining the fabric of hospitals: lack of money for maintenance in the past meant increased capital expenditure in the present; and maintenance in the present was often complicated (as was the contribution of ancillary services) by each section of the hospital staff owing primary allegiance to its own hierarchy.

It seemed then that nurse administrators, like hospital doctors, viewed the simpler problems of the past with some nostalgia: but at the same time, having been given greater responsibility for resource allocation, they saw greater possibilities of solving its problems within the existing hospital context. The key to their solution, one nurse administrator suggested, was a co-operative multidisciplinary approach by the different professions and specialities: this kind of approach, at the local level, made it easier to identify needs and priorities, and to make the best use of existing resources; but such an approach, many nurses felt, was only possible if the initiative was taken by the medical profession.

Nurses on the working group also suggested a number of specific resource allocation measures designed to save manpower costs. These included greater use of five-day wards and of hostel accommodation for well patients undergoing investigations. The latter, several members of the group pointed out, raised an interesting ethical question, since the main objection to such accommodation was fear of litigation (for example, in the case of a fire at night in an unsupervised hostel) while the advantages were not only financial but also moral, in that hostels avoided creating unnecessary dependency among well patients. Was this, some asked, a parable of the health service's larger problems, rooted in a bureaucratic paternalism transfixed by the fear of risk, and unwilling to admit that things could ever go wrong? The discussion once again had returned to the theme of honesty.

3) *The patient's perspective.* Honesty was also seen as a key factor when the working group considered the patient's perspective on resource allocation. Introducing the topic, one of the group's lay members agreed that many, perhaps most, laymen had an unrealistic view of medicine's possibilities. This was attributable not only to post-war optimism over advances in practical short-term medicine, but also to generally rising expectations during this period; in other words to the feeling of 'never had it so good' and the consequent belief that 'anything's possible'. It was attributable also to the average layman's ignorance of his own body: a university education, for example, was no guarantee that someone knew where his liver was, or what it was for; and the lack of formal education, on the other hand, was no longer any guide to the possession of practical folk-wisdom.

Optimism and ignorance then, created unrealistic expectations, and the desire for an ill-health service, to cure the disease at the moment when its symptoms arose. What most people seemed to want, in other words, were miracles: the 'breakthroughs' of the popular press, injections against cancer, community-funded trips to Russia or Switzerland for doubtful cures. The desire for miracles seemed much stronger than any desire for health education, which might obviate the need for them; and the desire was

sustained, in many cases, to the end, contributing to the con-
spiracy of silence, forced cheerfulness and heroic medical intervention which made for anything but a good death. Ultimately it
reflected a failure to recognise the essentially tragic element in
human existence.

Laymen were also unrealistic, if not irrational, in their assessment of their doctors. What many people wanted, it was suggested, was a personal doctor, someone to lean upon, preferably
kind but also authoritarian. Decisive doctors, wearing a collar
and tie, were commonly preferred to the more informal variety;
and with this in mind, one member of the group observed that
'patients who have bad doctors consider them marvellous: they
also tend to judge the system on this basis'. Nurses too were often
judged in less than rational terms: the image of selfless 'angels',
popular with some patients, was not unrelated to nursing effectiveness, but it also reflected the tendency to hyperbole of highly
vulnerable human beings.

Unrealistic expectations were often sustained in the face of
considerable evidence to the contrary, and what many patients
were prepared to put up with was remarkable. One of the most
common experiences, once the patient role had been adopted, was
of waiting—for admission to hospital, for investigations and
their results, for treatment and finally for recovery or discharge.
A great deal of this was unavoidable, but some of it was not:
mistakes could be made, individuals overlooked, tasks rather
than persons became the focus, routine took precedence over
everything else. Hospital tasks and routine were largely in the
patient's interest, but they also served as defence mechanisms
against the professionals' own anxiety; and while anxiety could
inhibit good care, small doses of it might stimulate the professional's imagination, in the patient's interest.

Most hospital patients, however, were unwilling or unable to
take active steps in their own interest. Some individuals, of course,
were remarkably aggressive towards general practitioners, and
professionals themselves, on becoming patients, were sometimes
demanding or critical of their treatment. But many professionals,
in their own sickness, were no less irrational than anyone else, and
most patients did not complain. The reasons for this were partly
cultural, reflecting the camaraderie of the stiff upper lip: but they
also had to do with the average patient's transient status and with
his vulnerability, putting the need to co-operate with the hospital
above all else. The rare cases of professional incompetence were
even more rarely recognised as such, and more rarely still com-
plained about, in Britain at least. Stoic silence in these cases

seemed to be the price of maintaining the effectiveness of the drug 'doctor'.

Silence did not imply consent, far less approval, however; and while some patients kept their complaints to themselves, others expressed them to their fellow-patients, frequently without the hope of any remedy. One lay member of the group reported a conversation with a patient whose recovery had been delayed as a result of complications unforeseen (or at least unexplained) by his doctor: the patient now accepted that doctors were not infallible, but it would have been easier to accept this, he remarked, 'if they did not pretend that they were'. Clearly, alongside the innumerable patients who consider their surgeons 'amazing' and their nurses 'angels', there are others who resent the dependent, depersonalised status too often awarded to patients. Another member of the group illustrated this from his own experience:

I had suffered a severe back-ache for a number of days. When this started to induce vomiting I decided to visit the hospital, not yet having registered with a GP. Within four minutes of completing a white card (most of the information seeming irrelevant—e.g. 'what is your religion?') I was naked, on my back in bed surrounded by curtains and completely powerless, my clothes having been removed in a bag. One hour later (desperate for the toilet) I called a nurse, who informed me that Doctor would decide when I could make that (by now essential) trip and offered me a urine bottle. Seemingly the risk factor of walking thirty yards became unacceptable immediately I became a 'patient'.

This member of the group evidently did not share the point of view of those laymen, mentioned earlier, who preferred authoritarian doctors; and the group as a whole recognised that almost anything it might say about the patient's perspective was subject to qualification. Some generalisations about the relationship between socio-economic status and patients' attitudes were no doubt possible: degrees of dependency and depersonalisation, after all, were experienced by many people at work as well as in hospital. But while such generalisations could be made and tested, it was not morally justifiable to draw implications for the care of patients simply from what the class they belonged to was accustomed to put up with. If the patient's point of view was to be considered in day-to-day resource allocation, the principle of respect for persons suggested that the differences between individuals, which constituted each patient's personality, were no less important than what they had in common.

Taking the patient's point of view seriously in resource allocation thus had daunting implications. Ideally, it involved the provision for each individual of technical resources and hotel accommodation at least as good as those available to the most affluent purchasers of Western private medicine. It also involved a degree of skilled care, attention and treatment normally achieved only by the most exceptional doctors and nurses. And even then, there was no guarantee that this was what the individual patient actually wanted: many, no doubt, would feel uncomfortable in a hospital which was too well appointed, others would prefer the kindly authoritarian surgeon with clumsy fingers, all perhaps, in the end, would still want miracles.

Neither miracles nor the ideal, in the group's opinion, were practical possibilities. The immediate prospect was not of progress towards such an ideal, but of an increasingly difficult struggle to maintain the standards which had been achieved, and perhaps, amid population growth and inflation, of declining standards. Under these circumstances, the best hope of maintaining standards without losing the confidence of patients and the public lay in what members of the group had already suggested — a policy of greater honesty.

What did this mean in practice? At one level it meant more and better health education, with the particular aim of discouraging unhealthy lifestyles and habits, such as smoking, which eventually precipitated disease. Some members of the group were sceptical about this, and doubted whether specific educational measures were ever likely to change individuals' habits very much: perhaps it was just human nature not to look too far forward, and then to expect miracles. Other members, however, pointed out that health education was still in its infancy, that it had never really been tried, and if, as some suggested, it was making some progress among the middle classes, that the rest of society might eventually follow their example. At the very least, schools could teach more about the body, its diseases, what could be cured, and what not; and education of this basic kind, all moralising apart, ought to have some beneficial effect, however limited.

On another level a policy of greater honesty could be pursued in the doctor-patient relationship. The group agreed that it was now of decisive importance for doctors to learn how to give patients an appropriate account, in simple language, of what was wrong with them and what they could do to help themselves. Some members of the group also believed that this should be extended to a more explicit contract of the kind often negotiated in psychiatry. The negotiation involved finding out what the patient felt he wanted and discovering how this could be matched with

47

what the staff felt the patient needed. If someone simply wanted a rest, and seemed to need it, this might be negotiated; but if he really wanted to be cured of being himself, then the doctor should try to explain to him that he must learn to live more effectively within his emotional means.

The group as a whole was sympathetic to the idea of contracts, and believed that these could reduce unrealistic expectations while giving patients greater responsibility for their own health. But several members expressed reservations about their practicability outside psychiatry. It would be difficult for a general practitioner or a surgeon, for example, to withdraw treatment on the basis of non-co-operation by the patient; and while contracts were desirable where practical, the idea of patient participation seemed to offer a more constructive approach. Meaningful patient participation required that the professional shared his knowledge with the patient, while also stating clearly the boundary lines where participation ended and professional decision-making took over. It also involved recognition and acceptance of risks, allowing patients to take decisions which the professional knew might end in failure. This idea also certainly raised serious difficulties, particularly among patients who were accustomed to others taking decisions on their behalf, or who were psychologically averse to decision-making, or who were simply too exhausted by illness. But even among the last, there were not a few who preferred the risk, even of major surgery, to the prospect of slow deterioration in dependency or pain. If only for their sake, the opportunity of participation should be offered.

Taking the patient's point of view seriously in resource allocation thus involved a policy of greater honesty, and in practice this meant better communication, both at the level of general education and at that of the doctor-patient relationship. Did it also mean greater participation by patients in planning and organising primary and hospital care? Some members of the group believed that it did, at least in general practice, and they commended the setting up of organisations on a model roughly analogous to parent-teacher associations. But other members were more sceptical about such developments: parent-teacher associations worked because parents had a long-term continuing interest in schooling, whereas most people on a general practitioner's list did not think of themselves primarily as patients, and if they did they were probably in no condition to be politically active. It was possible therefore that participation in such bodies might be left largely to those with personal grievances or to community activists; and if the latter, there seemed little point in adding to the existing provision for health boards or health councils. Greater public participation in health care decision making was certainly necessary if standards were to be maintained without losing the public's confidence. But a more fruitful approach to this might be either to make health boards more democratic or health councils more powerful.

EXCERPTS OF DISCUSSION

To illustrate the working group's deliberations in further detail the following edited excerpts from verbatim records of the working group's discussions have been supplied by Dr C.T. Currie. The excerpts are concerned with five key topics, which were also discussed on numerous other occasions: 'the comparison of need', 'personal responsibility in health', 'the limits of health care', 'who decides?' and 'the problem of priorities'.

The comparison of need. The first excerpt is of discussion following presentation of the paper on health economics which appears in the Appendix.

Social Worker. Can I make a naive point? There's an analogy between the economist in health care and the sociologist in the social services. He can define models you might apply to the pure situation, but if you do that without regard to the context it's no use. Economists are being asked to justify courses of action with no regard to the quality implications. These should be built in.

Economist. Yes: most work has been problem-solving. And I agree that there are major dangers in asking the economist to define the problems. Cost aside, the way you specify the model does bias the results. You leave out the imponderables because they are too difficult.

Physician. But it is legitimate to try. It should be seen simply as a 'dose-response' relationship. In the acute situation you get near this, but if you apply it to a social situation or to old people, you can't seem to distinguish the relationship between dose and response. Does that mean you get only a marginal response? And so does it matter, because the response is not directly related to the nature of the dose? The 'minimal response' can be achieved in a variety of ways—so choose the cheapest.

Economist. That may be true: but the same difficulties arise at the acute end too. Accepted treatments give major differences in results.

Physician. Then you just have to admit that there is a nil or minimum response. If you can't distinguish a 'dose-response' relationship, it means what you do doesn't matter.

49

Economist. But the social worker's point about the relevance of quality is important.

Community Physician. The really difficult value-judgment is when the 'quality of result' difference is minimal and the cost difference is large.

Physician. Then do it the cheaper way.

Economist. But that may be the cheaper way to the hospital, and at the same time the costlier way to the community and the family.

Social Worker. Yes. You can take a problem, find several solutions and apply the cheapest, but you need to do that from the national budget point of view and to look at the national effect. If you apply the cheapest solution in NHS terms, then the implications of costs to other sectors must also be taken into account. These, and the quality of variables are important. But they are also difficult to measure.

Physician. You can't get away from it—if it can't be measured, then it is not important, and you can't take it into account in decision-making.

Community Physician. It's just not as easy as that. Even when you count things, your information is not above suspicion. It's the same in the social services sphere, where superficial information is used dangerously.

Physician. What we're after is a single unit of comparison of need, universally applicable, something that you could go to the health board with.

Administrator. How about the decibel?

Personal responsibility in health. The second excerpt is concerned with the moral question of responsibility and with the nature of the doctor-patient relationship.

Community Physician. What about diseases where the life-style contributes to the disease process? To what extent can you hand back responsibility to the patient?

Hospital Doctor. Obesity is a good example: it increases the operative risk in elective surgery. There used to be a grand old surgeon round here who sent fat ladies with gall bladders away again and again until they came back thin.

Psychiatrist. You can make a contract with the patient: he has to keep his side, you keep yours. Or it may be something like the housewife going under—stress and poor personality. You take her in for a fortnight, virtually for a rest, and then she goes away and copes for another few months.

Community Physician. Yes, but what about when the life-style has done irreparable damage? We've got to take whoever comes along with a wrecked chest. You can't make a contract with him. It's too late.

Social Worker. And he would say, 'Look at the tax I've paid smoking for thirty years.' You can't opt out then. The doctor has to be honest and helpful and useful to the patient, whatever the circumstances.

Community Physician. Doesn't it come to education? If enough people knew, people wouldn't smoke. And people are stopping.

General Practitioner. Working-class women are smoking more.

Historian. Let's not be too pessimistic. Changes take generations. The evidence is that change is taking place.

Nurse. I only smoke in private now.

Administrator. What about a really hard line? Honesty. Statutory definitions of conditions, a, b, c and d, related to smoking. And then you could say, 'We're sorry the Health Service can't do anything for you.' It would make the consumer accountable.

General Practitioner. It's difficult. It's not as tidy as that. And as someone said earlier, you can't opt out.

The limits of health care. The third excerpt is concerned with whether the health service is making its own work unnecessarily difficult by creating expectations which it cannot possibly hope to live up to.

Historian. Are we drawing the boundaries in the right place between the medical (i.e. the technical, remediable) and the non-medical? Should we not think about reducing the perimeters of health care's ambitions? Perhaps one result of that would be less evaluation of non-evaluable items of service.

Community Physician. Health service activity does fall into various categories. There's medicine pure, and medicine mixed up with social work; and there's a large overlap with social work.

Physician. If it is curable it is medical. If you can prove it works it should be a universal provision. Coronary care units are a good example: you make pilot studies, you prove they work and then you make it a universal service.

General Practitioner. Coronaries are healthier at home. The company is better; but of course we often aim at treating people we can't treat.

Community Physician. One feels that the Health Service often ends up providing services inappropriate to the individual. And there is this very muddled trade-off with the social work department. Should we be dealing with them better, perhaps with some system of joint finance?

Social Worker. Look at attempted suicide. The social resources pour in. I'm not saying they do any good.

Psychiatrist. Attempted suicide has increased a hundred per cent over the last five years.

Administrator. Perhaps services attracted clients.

Physician. It's now very difficult to poison yourself successfully. Only one in a hundred needs extensive medical care. Most of them walk out after twenty-four hours at only trivial cost to the medical services. It's the follow-up, it's the social work that's expensive.

Psychiatrist. And there's no evidence of benefit.

Layman. Should we be trying to prevent suicide?

Social Worker. We feel that we must cope with everything. Perhaps we should be saying, 'this is my limit'; although that's easier in theory than in practice.

General Practitioner. Advice certainly doesn't help. Often you get a nil result after considerable effort. So do we simply say 'that's it', and leave it?

Hospital Doctor. Does one include alcoholism in this untreatable group?

Psychiatrist. Treatment is a complete waste of public money; perhaps we should stop pretending we're doing it.

Biologist. One can see what's wrong. Frustration, jealousy, lack of achievement: these are the problems of an overcrowded society, and why should the NHS pick up the tabs? The average person thinks that 'they' ought to do something, but why should they? It is the illusion of the West that the world owes us a living, and we expect too much. The message has to go out in an accessible, *Daily Record, Sun* sort of way.

Who decides? The fourth excerpt is from discussion at one of the hypothetical health board simulation exercises.

Community Physician. We've discovered that most of our budget is pre-committed, either to personnel or to existing projects. In the circumstances, what do we retain, postpone or cancel?

Administrator. On the operating theatre issue, does a new theatre reduce waiting lists?

Historian. Aren't waiting lists irreducible?

Physician. If the health board is like one I know, there are probably too many operating theatre facilities already. It's a problem of use, not provision.

Nurse. We ought to have more operational research: it's unethical to ask health boards to decide without it.

Physician. We don't want a horde of bureaucrats doing the

operational research. The best stuff is done by the professionals: for example the coronary care units. But it's also needed from geriatrics, from acute medicine and from surgery. That way you'd get a realistic discussion, but it's got to be within the profession. You need an inquisitorial committee, of bright disinterested chaps, something like a House of Commons Select Committee, filtering and eliminating axe-grinding and self-interest. But no bureaucrats. And another thing, you'd get the professionals free.

Administrator. You would still need bureaucrats.

Physician. What we want is good committees, tight intelligent committees, not lay people working *in vacuo*.

Administrator. To filter information for health boards?

Physician. Progress is made when an enthusiast can persuade his colleagues. But he has to make a good case. Take the examples of coronary artery surgery, ccu ambulances and genetic registers. All these are pushed by the professionals involved, and good cases are made.

Economist. Alright, but how do you decide between them?

Physician. Not by a lay board.

Administrator. At least they check costs.

The problem of priorities. The final excerpt is also from discussion during one of the health board simulation exercises.

Administrator. You can only say where the money goes. You can't say what it does. All those measurements of hospital bed-days tell you very little.

Accountant. They're not a measure of effectiveness or efficiency.

Community Physician. Let's say coronary artery surgery takes fifty patients a year and makes them better. Say half of them come off the dole. The surgeon, or the NHS, is simply saving someone else's money. The social work departments and the health boards end up playing Cox and Box. That happens in other areas. In general practice . . .

General Practitioner. You mean Family Planning? That was forced on us.

Social Worker. But what would you take out? Somebody ultimately has to take a decision, on attitudes and on inadequate information. Coronary artery surgery? Who would put a pen through that? Who would say: 'I accept the responsibility'?

Social Historian. It would be helpful to know . . .

Social Worker. I don't think expert opinion supplies the answer. In the big social work cuts in the region where I am, the experts simply said 'There's where you can make your cuts. That's what you can do. But you decide. You're the elected representatives.' And they had to cut services by £7½ million, and the decision on how to do it was political.

Accountant. Whatever your information, you have to make up your mind.

Acute Physician. If you have more information you have a better chance of making an honest titration of value. But that would be hard work, not the sort of thing for tired amateurs at the end of a hard day's work at something else. I suppose we do have government by amateurs, in various forms of democracy, and in jury service, but the price you pay is high.

Administrator. Perhaps we should train people for health boards.

Community Physician. People make decisions, big decisions, about other people's money all the time. Government does it, why shouldn't health boards?

Administrator. And still decision-making isn't information based. And giving more information may only make decisions more difficult, not necessarily better.

Health Economist. You can allocate needs into groups, for example those of the elderly, and then ask the proposers of these needs to allocate the priorities within these groups of needs, and then trade-off between them. That way you could combine the information and the political approaches.

Acute Physician. Take Beeching as an example of rational scientific management, as applied to railways. That sort of unemotional approach would appeal to the professionals.

General Practitioner. Railways are simpler to work out than health. How do you choose between the claims of the psychiatric and the renal dialysis patient? How do you convert need into allocation?

Acute Physician. You work out a system of weighted priorities. 1 equals indispensable to life, or hazard to staff. 2 is maintenance of the service as it stands. 3 is improvement of the service.

General Practitioner. What about prevention?

Acute Physician. You find some way of counting that too.

CONCLUSIONS

These examples of discussion from the working group do not take the form which the individuals concerned might have given them in a lecture or article, where inconsistency can be avoided by selecting the subject matter or the questions asked of it. The examples represent, rather, multiprofessional reflections from the raw edge of experience in the health care scene—which is and will doubtless remain a scene primarily of action and hence of some intellectual untidiness. For the purposes of this book, however, the members of the working group hoped that their reflections could also be presented in a more systematic and coherent fashion; and this was the task which occupied their last six months of discussion.

Part of the task, as already explained, was to discuss a series of papers prepared by the working group's secretary. The other part of the task was to produce a summary of the main areas of agreement and disagreement within the group: and although not all members were convinced that this would be possible, one member of the group, Dr Helen Zealley, succeeded in producing the following summary.

Summary
1) All health service activities should be monitored to ensure that only effective activities are continued on a mass scale.
2) Activities of unproven value, e.g. treatment of alcohol addiction and many cancers should be restricted to carefully controlled studies.
3) The provision of activities which are effective but very expensive should be limited to certain centres so as to reduce to a minimum their opportunity cost to other health care activities.
4) Priority should be given to 'rescue' activities that can save life and have the potential to restore a patient to a fully independent life.
5) Other possible health care activities of proven effectiveness should, where technically possible, be placed for every disorder in the following priority order:
   i. *Prevention*: e.g. Spina Bifida; Control of family size;
   ii. *Cure*, where prevention is not possible: e.g. So-called 'endogenous' depression; Hip replacement;
   iii. *Habilitation/Rehabilitation*, where prevention and cure are not possible: e.g. Mental handicap; Rheumatoid arthritis;
   iv. *Care*, where rehabilitation, cure and prevention are not possible: e.g. Dementia; Inevitable terminal processes.
   The scope for freeing resources from the latter activities (e.g. the case of children with spina bifida or adults with disabling osteoarthritis) to enable the highest possible activity to be promoted is limited unless agreement can be reached by the resources allocators on the ethical values they use to select priorities.
6) No priority should be afforded to minor self-limiting disorders except to promote the concept of responsibility for one's own health.

E 55

7) No agreement could be reached on the responsibility which should be assumed by the health care services for self-inflicted disease, e.g. caused by obesity or smoking.

8) Operational activities in the health service, e.g. the promotion of Health Centres, should be subject to similar monitoring arrangements as those for other health care activities.

Comment. After some examination by members of the working group this summary was generally agreed to. The significance of what was agreed to, however, bears some examination, best done perhaps by grouping the points made in four broad categories. First, (4) and (6) were those on which there was the most agreement within the group. In the summary these are stated in such a general, but carefully qualified, form as to make them at once incontestable and capable of considerable interpretation in practice. Second, (1), (2), (3) and (8), were points which two or three members of the group, but not more, might take issue with. In the summary these are stated in only a slightly less general form, and are again (with the exception of the first example in(2)) capable of considerable interpretation. Third, (5) is the point on which there was least agreement. In the summary this is stated in the least ambiguous way—although even here there is a caveat which leaves open one of the most basic questions (i.e. agreement on ethical values). Fourth, (7), as the summary states, was the point on which the group reached no agreement. This however was the issue which the group (which included smokers and non-smokers of varying weights) debated most often in explicitly ethical terms.

What emerges from this summary then, is a strong positive correlation between the amount of moral agreement within the working group and the amount of latitude permitted in its translation into practice. The extent of moral agreement therefore may not be so very great. To those accustomed to moral enquiry, this may not be very surprising: the Socratic dialogues themselves, after all, are often inconclusive. To those unconvinced of the value of such activity on the other hand, its apparent failure may suggest that it would be better simply to admit that resource allocation is a matter of politics and interest groups, and to act accordingly. This, however, would be to misunderstand both why moral enquiry is necessary, and how it relates to practical politics.

Why moral enquiry is necessary. That resource allocation is commonly a matter of politics can readily be agreed. Political conflict in fact is a prerequisite of good resource allocation, ensuring that the alternatives are exhaustively explored and our

liberties defended. Politics, however, cannot be adequately understood simply in terms of the interests of the groups involved in it:
intelligible and communicable purposes, conceived with common
as well as sectional interests in mind, also play a significant part
in politics; and thus there is some need not just for the cruder
forms of political horse-trading, but also for rational debate
about what is in the common interest or desired by the general
will.

Such debate, however, is not actively encouraged by the ritual,
conflict-based postures of contemporary politics. In the past,
particularly when political conflict was contained within a common moral framework provided by religion, law and tradition,
debate about purposes may have been less necessary. Today,
however, much of the common moral framework has disinte-
grated, and the survival of political government is at risk, not
only from bread and circuses political opportunism, but ultimately
from groups which seek to impose their ideology on society.
Under these circumstances, broadly-based moral enquiry, concerned with real-life conflicts (not, that is, just pressure-group or
academic moral enquiry) is needed, both to raise critical questions
about opportunism and ideology, and to sustain political government by expressing confidence in the possibility of rational agreement about political purposes.

How moral enquiry relates to practical politics. The claim that
moral enquiry is necessary may seem to be undermined, of course,
if moral enquiry repeatedly turns out to be inconclusive. This,
however, is to misunderstand its relation to practical politics.
The relationship is not one in which moral enquiry produces
answers which are then applied as solutions to political conflicts:
since neither politics nor ethics admit final solutions, the most
moral enquiry can do in this respect is to raise leading questions.
The important relationship rather is one in which moral enquiry
provides a form of continuing education for participation in
politics. In practice, that is, the experience of having to take
seriously, in rational debate, the variety of conflicting moral and
political judgments which others consider realistic, robs us of
recourse to the over-simplified solutions which we devise on our
own or with the like-minded. Like all good education, in other
words, moral enquiry is education into complexity; and its
success is to be measured, not in terms of the theoretical solutions
it provides, but in terms of the capacity it engenders for appropriate and effective action in the light of the largest number of
relevant considerations.

REFERENCES
1. Scottish Home and Health Department (1976) *The Health Service in Scotland: The Way Ahead.* Edinburgh: H.M.S.O.
2. Department of Health & Social Security (1976) *Priorities for Health and Personal Social Services in England.* London: H.M.S.O.
3. Department of Health & Social Security (1976) *Prevention and Health: Everybody's Business.* London: H.M.S.O.
4. *Public Expenditure to 1979–80* (1976). London: H.M.S.O.
5. Draper, P., Best, G. and Dennis, J. (1976) *Health, Money and the National Health Service.* London: Unit for the Study of Health Policy, Guy's Hospital Medical School.
6. Office of Health Economics (1975) *The Health Care Dilemma.* London: O.H.E.
7. SHHD (1976) *op. cit.* p. 1.
8. *ibid* p. 11.
9. *ibid* p. 16.
10. Draper *et al.* (1976) *op. cit.* p. 46.
11. *ibid* p. 53.
12. *ibid* p. 55.
13. OHE (1975) *op. cit.* p. 15.
14. *ibid.*
15. *ibid* p. 20.

CHAPTER 3

Historical Perspective

THE THREE following chapters of this report are an attempt to get
the moral problems of resource allocation into perspective, first
in historical terms, second in terms of some contemporary moral
arguments, and finally by asking if there is any way of making the
conflict between these arguments more creative and constructive.

The particular historical perspective outlined in the present
chapter is one which can open up when we ask: 'what is the
"good" of health care?' or 'what are medicine and society aiming
at?' The reason for beginning with this question is the obvious
one: amid the innumerable ambiguities, contradictions and self-
deceptions of any kind of human decision-making, it is often
instructive to ask ourselves what we were originally trying to do
before these difficulties arose. As far as health care is concerned,
our first thought may be that, in the past, medicine and society
knew very clearly what they were aiming at; and that with the
limited resources at their disposal, they went straight for it, so
that resource allocation was not really a problem. For many
practical doctors and nurses, no doubt this was the case: but that
does not mean that they were all aiming at the same thing, or that
changing ideas and circumstances did not affect their goals and
the ways in which they tried to reach them. In the rest of this
chapter therefore we shall trace, in the barest outline, some of the
more relevant ways in which ideas and circumstances changed,
and how eventually the basic problem of resource allocation in
health care today emerged.

PERSONAL CARE AND SCIENTIFIC CURIOSITY
The observation that health care practitioners in the past may not
all have been aiming at the same thing can be illustrated, at the
outset, by a passage from Plato's *Laws*:

Now here's another thing you notice. A state's invalids include
not only free men but slaves too, who are almost always treated
by other slaves who either rush about on flying visits or wait

59

to be consulted in their surgeries. This kind of doctor never gives any account of the particular illness of the individual slave, or is prepared to listen to one; he simply prescribes what he thinks best in the light of experience, as if he had precise knowledge, and with the self-confidence of a dictator. Then he dashes off on his way to the next slave-patient, and so takes off his master's shoulders some of the work of attending the sick. The visits of the free doctor, by contrast, are mostly concerned with treating the illnesses of free men; *his* method is to construct an empirical case-history by consulting the invalid and his friends; in this way he himself learns something from the sick and at the same time he gives the individual patient all the instruction he can. He gives no prescription until he has somehow gained the invalid's consent; then, coaxing him into continued co-operation, he tries to complete his restoration to health.

Make no mistake about what would happen, if one of those doctors who are innocent of theory and practise medicine by rule of thumb were ever to come across a gentleman doctor conversing with a gentleman patient. This doctor would be acting almost like a philosopher, engaging in a discussion that ranged over the source of the disease and pushed the inquiry back into the whole nature of the body. But our other doctor would immediately give a tremendous shout of laughter, and his observations would be precisely those that most 'doctors' are always so ready to trot you out. 'You ass,' he would say, 'you are not treating the patient, but tutoring him. Anybody would think he wanted to become a doctor rather than get well again.'[1]

This description of Greek doctors in the 4th-century BC is a good example to begin with for two reasons: it registers a change in the nature of health care which was taking place at that time; and it foreshadows changes which were to take place very much later.

The individual approach. The change taking place in the 4th-century BC and probably for about a century before that, was in the direction of what has been termed 'individualisation in treatment'.[2] The earliest human healers, medicine men in primitive societies, had been 'concerned not only with the people's health but with their entire welfare ranging from crops to victory in war';[3] and although medicine men took individual histories (in terms of offences committed, dreams, suspicious events and so forth[4]), their treatment was based on a blend of 'magical, religious and empirico-rational views and practices'.[5] Later healers, such as the priest-physicians of Babylonia and the scribe-physicians of Egypt began to shed some of the medicine man's multifarious but undifferentiated responsibilities. But here still, as in Greece until about the 5th-century B C, 'the physician appears as the dispenser of predetermined modes of practice, rather than the individual healer of his patients'.[6]

The arrival of the individual healer is reflected in the Hippocratic Oath, which was composed no earlier than the 4th-century B C,[7] and which presupposes the physician's personal responsibility for the treatment of his patients. The existence of Plato's 'free' doctors, who took this responsibility seriously in the individualised way he describes, is also referred to by Aristotle, who mentions three classes of doctor: 'the ordinary practitioner . . . the master of his craft, and . . . the man who has studied medicine as part of his general education'.[8] The first of these corresponds to the slave-doctors and the second to the free.

Cultural context. The causes and the consequences of the free doctor's individualised methods were alike significant. The causes, or at least the context, of his emergence may be seen in terms of cultural change between about 800 and 200 B C. This was a period of considerable social upheaval in the Mediterranean and Near Eastern world, and also the age of Old Testament prophecy, the teachings of Zoroaster, the Greek mystery cults and the rise of Socratic philosophy. During this period, it is often suggested, 'the idea of the autonomous responsible human being was born': and while this led on the one hand to belief in 'a desirable personal immortality',[9] it is also plausible to see it leading to the more personal medical practice of the 'free' doctor.

Scientific consequences. A further consequence of this era of course was a new spirit of intellectual enquiry; and in medicine the individualisation of treatment led in turn to the search for new theories, for the 'knowledge of what is healthy, diseased and neutral',[10] as Galen put it, without which treatment could not be fully effective. By the 1st-century A D therefore, medicine's commitment to science was great enough for the dogmatist sect to defend the vivisection of criminals with the argument that 'we should seek remedies for innocent people in all future ages'.[11] But as mention of the medical sects reminds us, much of the theoretical development of medicine from Hippocrates to Galen was more influenced by what we would now call philosophy rather than science; and the major contribution of Greek medicine to treatment was probably in more practical areas such as dietetics[12] and the development of scientific anatomy.[13] Nevertheless the Greek search for theory as a 'guide to the unknown' which 'allows individualisation in treatment'[14] had set up a medical ideal which still stands, enhanced today by its tantalising late fruits.

Just how late these fruits are is easily forgotten. The changes foreshadowed in Plato's description did not take place until very recently indeed. And when they did, they were complicated by other changes. We shall come to these other changes in a moment, but shall look at the late fruits first.

18th-century optimism. To do this we need go no further back than the mid-18th century. By that time, significant scientific advances had taken place, such as Harvey's discovery of the circulation, Sydenham's contribution to epidemiology, Hooke's introduction of the cell into microscopy and Boyle's work in chemistry. Actual treatment, however, was still based either on Galen or on trial and error.[15] And yet, with the decline of magical healing, which pre-dated the rise of scientific, a significant change had taken place. Again it reflected general cultural change, and we may think of it perhaps as an upward twist in the same historical spiral which the ancient medical sects had been trying to ascend. It was, one historian suggests, 'less a matter of positive technical progress than of an expectation of greater progress in the future. Men became more prepared to combine impotence in the face of current misfortune with the faith that a technical solution would be found.' They did this, he adds, 'much in the spirit in which we regard cancer today'.[16]

19th- and 20th-century achievements. Whatever happens in the case of cancer, the faith of the 18th century certainly seems to have been justified. Public recognition of a united and reformed modern medical profession was awarded by the 1858 Medical Act, passed a decade after Liston first used ether as an anaesthetic and a decade before Lister first used carbolic acid as an antiseptic. Public provision for health care, in the shape of the National Health Service, came at the end of a war in which Winston Churchill's life was saved by M & B 693 and the lives of many of his compatriots by penicillin. In the period between 1858 and 1958, increasing numbers of people in Britain survived infancy and into old age: fewer women died in childbirth, and rapidly decreasing numbers of the population died from cholera, tuberculosis, scarlet fever, diphtheria and other infectious diseases. The importance of sanitation and nutrition in the decline of many of these diseases, and the relative unimportance until quite a late date of specifically medical measures, now seems well established. But some medical men were deeply involved in sanitary reform and qualitatively if not quantitatively in improving nutrition (in the case of adulterated food, for example). Public confidence in the progress of orthodox medicine thus was not ill-founded, particularly in terms of its ability to save some from death and most from pain.

The possibility of medical effectiveness. These developments then can be seen as the late fruits of the spirit of personal care and scientific curiosity which the ancient Greeks pioneered; and by the middle of the 20th century it seemed as if medicine might now have the theoretical and practical equipment to put the Greek ideals into practice. At last, in other words, medicine had become effective; and in becoming effective it had become 'at one extreme so simple that appropriate action can be taken by rule of thumb, and at the other so complex that a doctor can do little without time, thought and the collaboration of doctors and other health workers'.[17] For many of the generation of doctors who entered practice during and just after the Second World War, this presented an ideal opportunity to work in the manner of Plato's gentlemen physicians, albeit scientifically and co-operatively. With the tools of technology and the assistance of other health workers, they could use this 'holistic and personal'[18] method to the maximum advantage, both in curing and alleviating many conditions of complex aetiology, and in preventing many other precipitated by environmental, social or behavioural factors.

The NHS and professional security. This prospect was enhanced, in one sense at least, by the advent of the National Health Service. The medical profession, it is true, had been granted a virtual monopoly in formal health care by the 1858 Act; and the other health professions and occupations were dependent on the doctor's clinical judgment. But elements of insecurity remained, and during the late 19th and early 20th centuries many doctors 'were still in the position of small tradesmen who had to do as instructed by the customer'.[19] In respect of clinical freedom therefore and also in terms of differential financial rewards within the profession, the NHS was to offer greater security to the average doctor, and particularly the general practitioner.

EPIDEMIOLOGICAL AND SOCIAL PROCESSES

Epidemiological and population change. It is somewhat ironic therefore that the NHS should also represent the culmination of another process of historical change which had made the possibility of medical effectiveness so difficult to realise. There are in fact two other historical processes involved here, a social one, which the NHS reflects, and an epidemiological. The latter we have already referred to when mentioning the decline of infectious diseases. The effects are well known: in practice they amount to a pattern of ill-health largely characterised by the chronic ailments of the old, diseases of middle life often precipitated by behavioural influences, and mental disorder among people of all ages. Although this pattern is not complicated in Britain by a population explosion on the scale being experienced in many poorer countries, the age structure of the population clearly has contributed to it. Those aged 65–74 comprised 3·3 per cent of the population of England, Wales and Scotland in 1901, but 7·97 per cent in 1966; while the proportion aged 75 and over rose from 1·4 per cent to 4·45 per cent during the same period.[20] By 1972 males over 65 and females over 60 represented 16·3 per cent of the total population, but were responsible for 28 per cent of NHS expenditure; and those over 75 were (by 1975) accounting for 29 per cent of all NHS bed use apart from psychiatric and maternity cases.[21]

This process of epidemiological and population change can be attributed in part to medical progress; but as we have already suggested, it probably owes much more to the rising standards of sanitation and nutrition of the last hundred years. Clearly it imposes many demands on the NHS, and equally clearly, success in one of the areas involved—prevention of the diseases of middle life—will probably serve to increase the demand in another—the care of the elderly. None of this, however, might make the ideal of medical effectiveness quite so difficult to realise, were it not that these developments have taken place in a democratic welfare state.

The organisation of health care: 18th century. This third process of historical change, of which the NHS reflects the culmination, is again relatively recent. Even as late as the 17th century 'the impact of organised medicine upon the lower reaches of the population', in England at least, 'was relatively superficial';[22] and although magical healing was rapidly declining in significance, household remedies were still widely used as the normal way of dealing with most sickness. A hundred years later things were little changed, although in the 18th century the rural population often came 'to rely in medical matters on the advice and assistance of educated lay persons',[23] such as the lord or lady of the manor or the parish priest.[24] Such indeed was the underdeveloped state of medicine at the time, that schemes were even suggested in several European countries (and actually tried out in Sweden) for a rural health service staffed by the parochial clergy. Linnaeus, one of several distinguished men who advocated this, wrote in 1751 that:

It would be of very great benefit to the state if most rural clergymen would understand how to cure the most common diseases, which destroy so many thousands of country folk every year. Most of them are easily cured like dysentry, scurvy, erysipelas, leg ulcers, acute fevers and intermittent fevers. All this knowledge can be learned by the students when they are at university within eight days at the most.[25]

Industrial and urban society. In England, schemes of this kind were not generally successful. In the late-18th century the number of apothecaries and Scottish-trained physicians was increasing and preparing the way for the 19th-century's new breed of general practitioners.[26] At the same time, the rural population was streaming into the new industrial and urban areas, where voluntary hospitals and dispensaries were also increasing in number. The movement towards a recognisable medical profession in what are now its familiar work settings had thus begun. As this movement developed the poorer sections of the population, having lost many of their old family and community support systems, became increasingly dependent on organised and orthodox health services. Sometimes of course they organised those services themselves, through Friendly Societies and other associations which employed doctors; and neither household remedies nor even some forms of magical medicine ever entirely died out. But the general trend was clear. In a largely industrial and urban society, where living standards were rising and democracy gradually being conceded, sickness insurance and eventually a national health service were seen as the way to ensure that 'comprehensive health and rehabilitation services for the prevention and cure of disease and restoration of capacity for work (were) available to all the community'.[27]

1945 and after. The Second World War was crucial to this third process of historical change. Britain, it has been suggested,

was the only nation state which went through the war from beginning to end to emerge victorious without marked political or social disturbance, and this fundamental stability made it possible for her to get on with the task of making society more equitable even while the war went on—although it would also ensure that its foundations would remain largely unchanged. What is more, the provision of the hope of this reconstructed community—which today we call the welfare state—became the essential requisite for the total participation in war of all its members, and a good deal of the national war effort was directed to the purpose of remedying the deficiencies of the past.[28]

The NHS then clearly was the realisation of long-held liberal hopes, whose essential realism conservatives from Bismark[29] onwards had recognised. With such widespread support it was inevitably an imperfect realisation. But what perhaps has made its imperfections so obvious today, is the fact that it was realised at the very moment when the possibility of medical effectiveness was glimpsed and the pattern of ill-health was changing.

CONFLICT AND TRUST

Conflicting expectations in health care. These three processes of historical change, medical, epidemiological and social, have transformed health care not just in Britain but, to different degrees in different countries, throughout the Western World as a whole. The trouble with those transforming agents, however, is that each has acted so quickly, and that acting together they have imposed considerable strain both on the doctor-patient relationship and on the body politic.

The strain imposed is seen in conflicting expectations and experience at the everyday level of health care. On the one hand, as we have already suggested, many doctors would like to practise rather in the manner of Plato's gentlemen physicians. But on the other, increasing numbers of people today think of effective health care as a right. The population as a whole of course has not taken over the aristocratic conception of the doctor as 'the highest class of body servant'; [30] and many people still do not object to the dictator-doctor as long as his orders succeed in 'fixing them up'. But the doctor is seen, increasingly, as a public servant, of whom the average patient has legitimate expectations; and increasingly these legitimate expectations are seen to include the right to know what is wrong, what the doctor proposes to do about it, and why.

Problems in the doctor-patient relationships. The problem about this from the average doctor's point of view is fairly obvious. He does not have the time to give everyone the kind of attention which a gentleman physician could give to gentlemen, particularly now that so much more is known about the nature of the body and of disease. So he is often forced to rush about, like Plato's slave doctor, but among patients who expect far more than Plato's slaves. And when, as he inevitably must, he fails to meet some of his patients' expectations, he is often criticised in terms which make him sound like an incompetent technician—or a bad slave doctor. All of this, naturally enough, is irksome for the doctor, who has inherited enough of the gentleman physician's status to dislike being assigned that of a technician, and who also, being human, dislikes letting his patients down.

Unfortunately this is not how it seems to all patients, particularly those whose doctors employ unhelpful receptionists, or frequently use night deputising services, or are said to have been seen on the golf course in the patient's hour of need. Nor is it how some people experience hospitals, where it was one thing to be kept waiting for charity, but another for your rights. And here too some of the workers are restive, from the consultant who ruefully concludes that 'when everybody's somebody, then no one's anybody' to the ancillary staff who, through industrial action, can realise the strength which complexity of organisation gives them. Rising expectations, in short, have made doctors and patients alike less tolerant of what once might have been put down to fate or inevitable human weakness. So it sometimes seems on both sides, happy exceptions notwithstanding, as if the doctor-patient relationship is coming under increasing strain, and as if the health service is being stretched to breaking-point by society's expectations of it.

'Doctor bashing' in perspective. All of this becomes particularly alarming, and not just to doctors, when it breaks out in acrimonious public debate, seen by one side as 'doctor bashing' or unreasonable demand on the health service, and by the other as a matter of defending the legitimate rights of patients and the public. There is of course nothing new in this. 'It is a sad commentary on human nature and social organisation that even in the midst of sorrow and suffering when there were lives to be saved and pain to be alleviated, bureaucratic wrangling should have had so much effect on the efficiency of the hospital service',[31] Cipolla writes, commenting on the failure of the Prato hospital *della Misericordia*, in 1630, to send help it could well afford to plague victims in the city pest-house. And the 'prevalence of illiberality in country towns and villages; and jealousy existing between individual practitioners, who frequently, under the mask of candour and professed friendship, undermine each other's reputation, and never lose a chance of sinking one another in public estimation, when this can be done with seeming good grace and kindness'[32] was remarked upon by Abraham Banks in 1839. So if anyone is surprised by acrimonious public debate about health care, it can only be because his historical memory is short—or perhaps because his expectations of public administration and debate, like everything else, have been affected by inflation. Nevertheless, the fact that it is unsurprising makes it no less alarming.

The question of trust. What is alarming about such acrimonious public debate, particularly when health care workers are seen to be quarrelling among themselves, and even more when patients' representatives start taking sides against doctors, is that trust, on which even scientific medicine still largely depends, is put at risk. The question of trust, between doctor and patient, between health workers themselves, and between medicine and society, may thus legitimately be seen as the hidden agenda of contemporary debate about scarce resources in health care.

Health care then has been transformed by medical technology, changing patterns of ill-health and democratic affluence. In a situation where medicine is doing far more for far more people, health workers included, far more still expect far more yet. Rising expectations, conflicting, create tensions which ultimately put trust and hence the whole enterprise at risk. These then are the circumstances which have made the problem of resource allocation in health care today so difficult and so pressing.

REFERENCES

1. Plato, *The Laws*, Book 4, 720, 857. Harmondsworth: Penguin Classics, 1972 (translated by T. J. Saunders).
2. Temkin, O. (1977) *The Double Face of Janus and Other Essays in the History of Medicine*, chapter 8, p. 248. Baltimore: Johns Hopkins University Press.
3. Sigerist, H. E. (1967) *Primitive and Archaic Medicine* II, 5, p. 161. New York: Oxford University Press.
4. *op. cit.* II, 6, p. 181.
5. *op. cit.* II, 7, p. 209.
6. Temkin (1977) *op. cit.* chapter 2, p. 42.
7. *vide* Edelstein, L. (1967) 'The Hippocratic Oath: Text, Translation and Interpretation', *Ancient Medicine* pp. 3–63. Baltimore: Johns Hopkins.
8. Aristotle *Politics* III, 6; 1282 a, Loeb Classical Library (translated by H. Rackham).
9. Hick, J. (1976) *Death and Eternal Life*, chapter 3, 4, p. 67. London: Collins.
10. Temkin (1977) *op. cit.* chapter 2, p. 42.
11. *ibid* fn. 6.
12. *op. cit.* chapter 8, p. 148.
13. *op. cit.* chapter 2, p. 42.
14. *op. cit.* chapter 8, p. 148.
15. Poynter, F. N. L. and Keele, K. D. (1961) *A Short History of Medicine*, chapter 4, p. 52f. London: The Scientific Book Club.
16. Thomas, K. (1973) *Religion and the Decline of Magic*, chapter 22, 3, p. 790. Harmondsworth: Penguin Books.
17. Ellis, J. R. (1976) *Human Values in Medical Education*, p. 10, Philadelphia, Society for Health and Human Values.
18. *ibid.*
19. Klein, R. (1973) *Complaints against Doctors*, chapter 3, p. 62. London: Charles Knight.
20. Halsey, A. H. (ed.) (1972) *Trends in British Society since 1900*, Table 2.4, p. 33. London: Macmillan.
21. Cooper, M. H. (1975) *Rationing Health Care*, p. 18. London: Croom Helm.
22. Thomas (1974) *op. cit.* chapter 1, p. 14.

23. Heller, R. (1976) ' "Priest-doctors" as a rural health service in the Age of Enlightenment', *Medical History*, 1976, vol. 20, no. 4, p. 362.
24. *vide* (ed.) Paul, J. B. (1922) *Diary of George Ridpath, Minister of Stitchel 1755–1761*. Edinburgh: Scottish History Society (Third Series, Vol. II).
25. Heller (1976) *op. cit.* p. 365.
26. Waddington, I. (1977) 'General Practitioners and Consultants in Early Nineteenth-Century England: A Sociological Analysis, *Health Care and Popular Medicine in Nineteenth Century England*, ed. Woodward, J. and Richards, D., chapter 6. London: Croom Helm.
27. Watkin, B. (1975) *Documents on Health and Social Services 1834 to the present day*, 3.2, p. 80. London: Methuen & Co. (quotation from Beveridge Report, 1942).
28. Birch, R. C. (1974) *The Shaping of the Welfare State*, chapter 8, p. 47. London: Longman.
29. *vide* Sigerist, H. E. (1943) 'From Bismark to Beveridge: Developments and Trends in Social Security Legislation'. *Bulletin of the History of Medicine*, vol. XIII, 1943, pp. 365-388.
30. Magee, B. (1977) *Facing Death*, p. 212. London: William Kimber.
31. Cipolla, C. M. (1973) *Cristofano and the Plague*, p. 82. London: Collins.
32. Banks, A. (1839) *Medical etiquette*, p. 39, London: Charles Fox (quoted in Waddington, I. (1975) 'The Development of Medical Ethics—A Sociological Analysis', *Medical History*, 1975, vol. 19, p. 40).

CHAPTER 4

Contemporary Perspectives

THE LAST CHAPTER set the problem of resource allocation in historical perspective, but that is not the only perspective in which it can be viewed. Others, broader or narrower, related to the interests or purposes of individuals or groups, their day-to-day preoccupations or their long-term hopes and fears for the future, also influence how the problem is understood. This chapter examines four such perspectives, describing them in terms not so much of what health care is aiming at, as of the right way to use and distribute resources.

Questions about the right use and distribution of resources can be answered in a variety of ways. The different answers different people give can range from 'Follow me around and keep your eyes open' to 'There are five standard conceptions of social justice, and we may begin by considering . . .'. In this chapter we shall attempt to steer a middle course between these two approaches, in the belief that this will be closer to the kind of argument people with practical experience of the subject advance in open discussion.

The arguments described and criticised in this chapter do, in fact, reflect some of those used by members of the working group on the ethics of resource allocation. For the present purpose, however, we have conflated some, sharpened up others, and in some cases introduced elements of an argument which no members of the working group advanced quite so strongly. This has been done in the hope that what was always a lively and acutely intelligent set of discussions, in which the practical implications of theoretical distinctions had continually to be checked out, may not be entirely lost on the printed page. Four kinds of argument will be considered, which we have termed respectively: 1, Ecological and Epidemiological; 2, Clinical; 3, Administrative; and 4, Egalitarian.

70

ECOLOGICAL AND EPIDEMIOLOGICAL ARGUMENTS

A precarious equilibrium. Ecological arguments reflect the concern of many biologists with the earth itself as a limited resource. Man, so this kind of argument goes, shares the planet with three to four million other types of living organism, between which stability is maintained by competition for limited resources, the competitors including disease-bearing microparasites. An American historian, stretching the analogy, has suggested that:

> one can properly think of most human lives as caught in a precarious equilibrium between the micro-parasitism of disease-organisms and the macro-parasitism of large bodied predators, chief among which have been other human beings.[1]

This precarious equilibrium, however, the argument continues, has been upset by man, and particularly in the last three centuries by his improved agricultural and medical technology, which has enabled him to step outside traditional constraints. Success in what the same author calls 'the race between skills and ills'[2]—the skills being mostly medical, the ills infectious disease in particular —is now exposing man to the new risk of overpopulation in relation to food supplies and other natural resources. Having achieved death control, for the time being, will man succeed in achieving birth control, and hence some degree of equilibrium?

Not, it is answered, if he, and Western man in particular, persists in his present dangerously irrational attitude to medicine. The success of medical skills in recent centuries has led him to think of medicine as if it were magic, relieving him of responsibility for his own health, and deceiving him about life's character as a condition with 100 per cent mortality. Through this attitude to medicine, man is progressively disabling himself in his struggle for survival, and in order to save him from himself, a much more modest and realistic attitude must be cultivated by both medicine and government. Specifically, priority should be given to the kind of health education which creates among individuals a greater awareness of and sense of responsibility for their own physical welfare. Priority should also be given to the promotion of birth control; and research and development in medical science should be geared to whatever helps restore a greater degree of equilibrium between man and other forms of life.

Arguments based on ecological criteria then, interpret humanity today as 'in course of one of the most massive and extraordinary ecological upheavals the world has ever known'.[3] Estimates of the consequences vary from the sober ('a sequence of sharp alterations and abrupt oscillations in existing balances between micro-parasitism and macro-parasitism', i.e. disease and war, 'can . . . be

F   71

expected in the near future as in the recent past') [4] to the frankly pessimistic—often expressed by comparing mankind with lemmings. The message of many ecologists, with its overtones of judgment and nemesis, is thus at least as ancient as Hebrew prophecy and Greek myth. In its vision of an ominous future, there is little room for concern with the redistribution of health care resources on a fairer basis. It is not that ecologists do not consider a fairer distribution desirable, simply that they want to win the battle of El Alamein before they sit down to read the Beveridge Report.

Epidemiological optimism. The prospect of a long battle, with many casualties, is also accepted by others who read similar augures from the point of view of epidemiology. Seeing nutrition and hygiene as key factors in the decline of infectious diseases, aware of the threat of overpopulation, but rather more appreciative of the contribution medical science has and may yet make to saving lives and relieving pain, they take a less pessimistic view than the grimmer ecologists. 'The idea that pain and suffering are inevitable is I think mistaken', one epidemiologist writes; and he goes on to point out that 'with the provision of sufficient food and control of hazards in the past few centuries, many people have completed their lives without severe or prolonged physical discomfort'. [5]

The grounds for optimism about the future, in this kind of epidemiological perspective, lie in the possible success of measures similar to those proposed by the ecologist. Overpopulation, and diseases brought on by environmental and behavioural factors are the major risks to the race and individuals respectively. The remedy is twofold: intensified research into the determinants of disease and intensified effort in finding ways of changing reproductive and disease-precipitating behaviour. The aim, in short, is to be as sure about other causes as about smoking, and to stamp them out.

Epidemiologists and others who take this line, of course, are not naive: they realise it will be difficult, and their guarded optimism springs more perhaps from their personal and professional commitment to the task than from any evidence that medical science will be as intelligent or the population as rational as they suggest. Nevertheless, the best hope, as they see it, lies in a shift of emphasis away from traditional biomedical research to epidemiological, and from acute interventionist medical care to health education, environmental medicine, and long-term health care of the sick and disabled.

Ecologists and epidemiologists alike then, seem to be calling for a less Promethean posture from medicine, and a more responsible and rational response from the public in general. As far as the distribution of resources is concerned, the epidemiologists are concerned not so much with social justice, as with a distribution which does fairer justice to the balance of health needs today, as they see them.

Criticism of the kind of arguments based on ecological and epidemiological criteria can be levelled from at least three quarters. First, it can be suggested that the ecologists are too pessimistic for anybody's good: if the situation is as bad as they suggest, what is the point of trying to do anything about it? Why not let nature take its course? To this, of course, the ecologists may well reply that nature will, but what is the point of prophecy?

Second, in criticism of the epidemiological version, it can be suggested that the redistribution of resources this proposes, (a) misunderstands the role of medicine and (b) is unrealistic about human nature. These criticisms are best accounted for in terms of the positive clinical alternative to which we shall turn in a moment. A third criticism is that the epidemiologist's proposed redistribution within health care is particularly unrealistic about human nature because it discusses the task in isolation from the wider problem of radical social change; but this criticism too is best accounted for in terms of the positive egalitarian alternative, to be discussed below. For the present, however, it should be said in defence of epidemiologists, that they are not unaware of or unconcerned with the problems of social inequality.[6]

A CLINICAL ARGUMENT

A matter of judgment. Clinicians, like ecologists and epidemiologists, are not all of one mind—as the advocates of randomised controlled trials and medical audit are quick to point out. So in referring to clinical criteria here, we are not suggesting that all or even most clinicians would subscribe to the kind of argument outlined below, which is essentially a moral argument drawing on the clinical context for inspiration and illustration. Advocates of this kind of argument, of course, may suggest that it is essentially scientific or biological. But like all the arguments outlined in this section it is prescriptive as well as descriptive, and its truth is a matter of judgment rather than proof. It seems more accurate therefore to think of the argument as moral rather than biological and broadly philosophical rather than narrowly scientific.

The clinical argument we are concerned with here again involves an interpretation of mankind's recent history and its involvement with the development of modern medical skills. This recognises

73

the ecologist's and epidemiologist's doubts and fears about over-population and environmental and behavioural influences on health today. But, like the gloomier ecologist, it pins little hope on the epidemiologist's remedies. In terms of the time-scale involved, disease patterns may well change before the determinants of many current diseases have been isolated. And in the unlikely event of human habits having changed in the direction desired by the epidemiologists, who is to say that the new habits engendered will be functional in terms of the fresh challenges posed by new diseases? In practice, of course, medicine should not give up the attempt to persuade people to stop smoking, take more exercise and control their reproductive behaviour. But on the other hand it should not labour under the illusion that preventive medicine and health education will ever lighten its curing and caring load. In so far as he fosters this illusion it is the epidemiologist who is being Promethean and heroic in his attitude to medicine.

The clinical argument then is that the epidemiologist's redistribution of resources is based on speculative arguments from uncertain premises. Current critics of clinical practice may be correct in saying that the potential benefits of medical progress have been oversold, that medicine is too often seen as a new kind of magic, and that this has allowed overmuch investment in therapies of unproven value. But this is no justification for diverting resources to activities whose value is not only unproven but unprovable. A better alternative clearly, is to concentrate on what medicine can do, and ensure that it does it better.

Saving life and curing sickness. What medicine can, and should do, according to the clinical argument, is to save life and cure sickness. Survival in life-threatening circumstances is the first priority shared by the medical profession and the public; and the second priority is cure, in the 17th-century sense[7] of recovery from acute illness through treatment. Medicine of course cannot save every life it tries to save; and biological survival can be secured at too great a cost in terms of human survival. Many people, once cured, may enjoy suboptimal levels of health; and many cures may literally be short-lived. Nevertheless, in the attempt, medicine gives of its best and the public are best satisfied. As a scientific enterprise medicine is committed to a belief in therapeutic progress. As a humane art it is committed to a belief in the equal value of all human life. Under these circumstances it would be wrong to suggest that cures which prolong life for only a few years are some sort of second best, and it would be foolish to divert resources away from the search for better cures.

Prevention, after all, seems better than cure only to those for whom it works.

But can we afford better cures when already the most marginal improvements are so expensive? The question of total expenditure, and of the relative amounts to be spent on cure and care, the clinical argument suggests, are matters for the politicians to decide, after sounding both public and medical opinion. Their decision, unless influenced by ideologues, is likely to continue to give high, although not exclusive priority to life-saving and sickness-curing measures. It is even more likely to do so if bio-medical scientists and clinicians use the resources they are given as efficiently and effectively as possible; and this can be ensured by the exercise of scientific intelligence and clinical judgment.

Centres of excellence. What this means in practice is that research and development in medicine should be carefully monitored, and each new line of investigation and therapy restricted to a few selected centres of excellence. Laboratory (and for that matter epidemiological) research should be instigated in consultation with clinical practice, and new therapies demonstrated to be both efficient and effective before being generally adopted. Where this has been done in the past, initially expensive therapies, once shown to be effective, have been developed and refined so as to make them, eventually, widely available at greatly reduced cost. Conceptual difficulties, of course, can be raised about the measurement of effectiveness, but given the equal value of all human lives, a realistically limited idea of cure, and a consideration of the alternatives, these present fewer problems to the practitioner than to the theorist.

The clinical argument rests, at this point, on profound faith in the scientific intelligence, clinical judgment and common sense of medical scientists and practitioners. Evidence to the contrary, about wasteful research and the widespread use of ineffective therapies is not seen as a major problem. It is simply part of the pattern of medical progress to make some mistakes, and the way in which some scientists and clinicians behaved during the late era of generous funding will be understandable to anyone who has ever received an unexpected legacy. Tighter budgets now mean tighter controls, but not a major change of direction.

Expensive mistakes, like coronary care units, will wither away, perhaps in a decade. But the process of medical progress is big enough to learn from its mistakes, and to adjust its sights accordingly. The idea that it will not, is simply a species of what has been called the classic liberal fallacy 'that things are always about to go wildly out of control'.[8]

The clinical argument admits that its prescriptions make little contribution toward a fairer distribution of health care resources, either between the care and cure sectors, or between advantaged and disadvantaged nations, regions, classes and individuals. But, it argues, the existence of temporary inequalities between the two sectors, (and to some extent between nations and regions) acts as a stimulus to progress, both in terms of medical motivation and in terms of public opinion. And on past evidence, it claims, the controlled development of scientific medicine is likely to be accompanied by progressively rising levels of general health care. What is not likely, and what in political terms is highly unrealistic to hope for, is that resources diverted away from the cure sector will find their way to improving levels of care.

Random selection for treatment. Another aspect of this clinical argument about the distribution of resources, may or may not be held in conjunction with the position just outlined. This concerns the question of how to treat individuals fairly in the process of medical progress, and particularly when new therapies of relatively well proven effectiveness are still not generally available to all who could benefit from them.

One way of handling this problem is by constructing a checklist of clinical and social factors in terms of which each individual's claims can be measured. An obvious example of where this could be used is in the selection of patients for kidney machines.[9] The particular clinical argument we are concerned with here, however, rejects this option for three reasons: first, by offering a 'solution' to this problem of scarce resources it reduces the stimulus towards making dialysis more widely available at less cost; second, the procedure proposed involves too many subjective criteria to be workable; third, it does not take sufficiently seriously each individual's equal right to life and health. The only policy in such cases which meets all these objections is one of random selection, or first come first served, among those potential patients who are not excluded from the outset by clinical criteria, i.e. by the reasonable likelihood that they will not respond to the treatment.[10]

In criticism of this argument, it can be suggested that a policy of first come first served is not as random as it may appear. While, under the NHS at least, poverty is no bar to expensive life-saving treatment, it is at least possible that members of the higher social classes and the more intelligent members of all classes will make use of the health service in ways which bring them to the point of selection sooner than the socially and educationally disadvantaged. It is also possible, having arrived at this point, that the advantaged will appear less unsuitable even in clinical terms, both in relation to their health history and in relation to their motivation to respond to treatment. These considerations may make the separation of clinical and social criteria more difficult than at first sight.[11] In doing so, however, they do not necessarily invalidate the random selection argument, since much of its force lies in the question of whether a better alternative can be proposed.

General criticism. In criticism of the general clinical argument about the use of resources, three points can be made. First, its assumption that the epidemiologist's option is unrealistic, may itself be unrealistic. It may well be, in other words, that the health problems left by the receding tide of infectious diseases are radically different to those known to previous generations, and that a society itself changed by the influence of mass education and democracy can respond to this challenge in the manner the epidemiologist hopes for.

Second, it may be that the clinical argument's assumption about medical progress itself rests on too narrow a premise. The experience to which it appeals may well be that of an atypical era in human history. Medical progress during the last hundred years, that is, may represent the ascent from a plain to a plateau, rather than the foothills of a mountain of health. Its hope of further progress through controlled medical research and development, and of widespread therapeutic benefits eventually available at reduced cost, in other words, may be illusory.

Third, inequality in health care may not be as inevitable as the clinical argument supposes. An important part in this argument is played by the idea that inequality acts as a stimulus to progress. But if increasing numbers of people begin to find the two previous criticisms of the clinical argument plausible, it is not impossible that the best minds in medicine will turn to epidemiology and the 'care' section, and that the public will begin to think of progress more in terms of preventive measures and the equalisation of care. More about equalisation will be said below in outlining the administrative and egalitarian arguments. For the moment, the point previously made about criticism of the random selection argument can simply be repeated in connection with criticism of the clinical argument in general. The advocate of the clinical argument remains to be persuaded that a better and more realistic alternative has yet been proposed.

AN ADMINISTRATIVE ARGUMENT

Respect for realism. The administrative argument we are concerned with here (again, needless to say, not an argument which all administrators would accept) begins with an admission of respect for what it sees as the realism not only of the clinical argument, but also of the epidemiological—at least in so far as the latter talks of present realities, like observable changes in patterns of disease and changes in the age structure of the population. Realism and a concern for the present and the possible are leading features of this administrative argument; and because of this it is critical as well as appreciative of the clinical and epidemiological arguments.

Its criticism concerns not so much what these arguments say as what they leave out, principally about the distribution of resources. This, the administrative argument suggests, is what it may be able to supply. 'Administration', after all, means not only the management of business, but also 'the bringing of comfort to' and 'the application of justice'.[12] These ethical values, which good administration embodies, need to be emphasised in health care today, since comfort is not always brought to those who need it, nor available resources distributed between geographical regions, between specialities and between classes of sufferers, with a sufficient measure of justice.

The health service industry. The administrative argument about how this should be remedied is expressed in terms of its view of health care primarily as a matter of health services. Informal self-care and community care are of course recognised as significant elements in the scene, and the provision of health education is seen as important. But their significance and importance are difficult to predict and quantify, and so the argument's interest in them is to some extent rhetorical and peripheral. Its central concern is what it sees as the health service industry, although it does not always call it that.

The health service, it is of course admitted, is a unique industry with a unique product. But this unique product was, for generations, either bought and sold in the marketplace or (in the case, for example, of public health and some hospitals) administered as a charity. Today, in Britain at least, the industry has been nationalised, and anyone who needs its product is in principle entitled to it. But the product is increasingly expensive to produce, and the money needed to run the industry is limited. What is required therefore, is a fair system of rationing the resources available.

The fairest system, according to the argument, is one which ensures that basic needs are met, including the basic health needs of the population and the reasonable employment needs of health care workers. Such a system, the argument continues, is difficult but not impossible to devise. The primary requirement is to get more information about the groups and conditions requiring service, the numbers to be served, the nature and degree of need, the manpower resources and facilities available, the kind of activity required (e.g. hospital admission, outpatient attendances, day care or home visits), the cost of all these factors and their relative effectiveness and efficiency.[13] Not all this information of course will ever be fully available, nor is it all necessary. But enough needs to be gathered to construct a reasonable calculus of probabilities, on the basis of which rational decisions can be taken about which groups and which conditions should get which resources, within the overall financial and manpower restraints.

A calculus of this kind, naturally, will never be perfect; and it will need continual revision and refinement by economists and other experts. But if the best brains are employed in the task, and the maximum relevant and available data collected, rationing on this basis can be defended as the fairest and most efficient method of bringing comfort, in the form of health care, to a population which presumably wishes to see good stewardship of its resources. In a similar manner, a comparable end can be sought in the case of regional inequalities, by constructing information-based revenue equalisation models, perhaps along lines like those suggested by the current Resource Allocation Working Parties.[14] And in the long run, it may be possible to include in the calculus some provisions for categories which allow the patient or client to assess their own health care needs.

The sophisticated techniques required for this last possibility, the administrative argument continues, probably lie some way in the future. But they are mentioned here as an earnest of the argument's intention, which, through refining the rationing system, is to press continually towards a distribution of resources which is not only efficient, effective and fair, but also seen to be so.

At this point, however, the administrative argument admits some difficulties. The task of devising a rational rationing system, which the public will recognise as reasonable, is complicated by two factors. On the one hand, the money needed to run the industry, although always limited, comes in fits and starts, depending upon how politicians manage and interpret the economy; and sometimes it comes with strings, when politicians make political decisions about health care priorities. On the other hand, the workers are not entirely co-operative either. In framing the categories and gathering the information for the rationing calculus, the assistance of doctors and other health workers is indispensable. But even in connection with relatively simple matters, like controlled trials and medical audit, many of them seem unwilling to have their treatment and performance assessed, claiming that these are matters of clinical judgment. Can it therefore be assumed, with any degree of optimism, that they will co-operate any better in the larger task ahead?

The administrative argument gives no very clear answer to this last question, and seems to proceed hereafter on the assumption that its own proposals are so inherently rational that the workers must eventually recognise this and come into line. Its doubts about the inherent rationality of politicians, or at least of the political system, are more serious however. Some hope, it suggests, may lie in decentralising decision-making to local levels where ideological conflict may be less obtrusive. But the argument on the whole subscribes to Mill's dictum: 'Power may be localised, but knowledge, to be most useful, must be centralised';[15] and it sees little option to a system in which appropriate decisions have to be taken at regional and national as well as local levels.

Under these circumstances it seems unlikely that political interference with the administration of health services can be avoided. It can however perhaps be minimised; and the best way of doing this may well be by administrators and planners continuing their pursuit of rational rationing systems, in the hope that these will eventually seem more acceptable to the public and politicians alike than the ideological alternatives.

Alongside this activity of course the efficient management of health services must continue. The best stewardship of resources thus involves the maintenance of the industry's present output, together with every effort, whenever political and economic circumstances are favourable, to distribute the product more fairly among those who both need and are entitled to it. Regrettably, the argument concludes, this requires a degree of administrative opportunism, and the adoption, at the end of a period of 'disjointed incrementalism', of a policy of disjointed equalisation.

Criticism. Among the criticisms which can be made of this kind of administrative argument, two will be mentioned when we consider the egalitarian option which follows. These are concerned with (a) whether the administrative notion of justice is adequate and (b) what difference there is between this kind of administrative system and the political system it is so suspicious of. Other criticisms which could be raised concern: (c) whether a nationalised industry (however unique) is the best model for thinking about health services; (d) whether the notion of identifiable basic health needs is not much too relative to be of much use, and whether it would not in fact produce a very low base line;

and (e) whether the sophisticated techniques needed to produce a fair rationing system (assuming the experts can agree and the data can be collected) are not too sophisticated for the public and indeed politicians to see (rather than believe) that justice is being done.

We shall not, however, attempt to answer these questions here, but instead ask another. Taking into account both the administrative argument's reliance, for justification, upon the future, and its capitulation, in the present, to a degree of opportunism, is it really an argument at all? Is it not, rather, a series of increasingly ambitious and obfuscating rationalisations for an activity which one anonymous but senior health service administrator recently admitted was conducted, typically, 'at the level of the spinal reflex'?

This criticism of the administrative argument may well be fair. The attempt to manage business, bring comfort and apply justice in a single process sandwiched between politics and practice, may in fact involve too many self-contradictions to allow rational justification. But the administrator, as a 4th-century BC Brahman practitioner of the art once put it, knows that 'the life of a man under the service of a king is aptly compared to life in a fire'.[16] And asking whether the three values of administration are ones its critics would wish to see abandoned, he may well have the last word, in the form of the administrator's traditional question: 'What is the alternative?'

AN EGALITARIAN ARGUMENT

If the egalitarian argument we have in mind had to answer the administrator's question, it would probably be by telling him to try harder. This argument's goal is 'a society based on principles of real caring and real equality'[17] in which the cycle of multiple deprivation no longer drags the poor downwards. Its suspicion of the administrative argument, and for that matter the clinical and even the epidemiological, is essentially that they are not sufficiently in earnest about this central problem of our society.

The egalitarian argument's criticism of the epidemiological and administrative arguments is that neither goes far enough in its diagnosis and prescriptions. The epidemiologist's concern with health education, environmental medicine and long-term care of the sick and disabled is admirable: self-care should be encouraged and people should take responsibility for their own health. The problem, however, is that it is the middle classes, who know how, and are able, to help themselves, who will benefit from such developments rather than the poor. Without a more radical transformation of society, through which everyone can take responsibility not just for their health but for their living and working conditions in general, the epidemiologist's cure cannot be applied to those who need it most.

The argument's criticism of the administrator is similar. His concern to distribute comfort fairly to different regions, specialities and groups of sufferers again is admirable. But his discussion of these inequalities 'is too often sealed off from the discussion of the underlying inequalities of class, income and housing and living conditions created in our market economy'.[18] These underlying inequalities are reflected in the radically worse sickness and death rates of the poor, evidence for which is now too well established by statistics to dispute.[19] They are also reflected in evidence which, although more difficult to interpret, 'suggests on the whole that the amount of use and effectiveness of use of the different parts of the health service varies with social class and generally speaking in the direction of less use being made as we go down the social scale'.[20]

The criticism of ignoring the social facts is also applied to the clinical argument, and in particular to its defence of random selection. But in criticising the clinical argument, the egalitarian strikes deeper, seeking a reason why epidemiologists, clinicians and administrators alike are not sufficiently committed to solving the problem of poverty and social deprivation. This reason it finds in what it considers the professional's divided attention on the subject. On the one hand he subscribes to an ideology of caring, in many cases quite genuinely. But on the other he is concerned 'to secure high status as a guarantee of autonomy'.[21] The professions thus, while embodying important social and moral values, and generally doing a great deal of good, also betray

> tendencies to monopolise technical know-how, establish dogmas of omniscience, omnipotence or infallibility, protect members against outside criticisms, use power to secure excessively privileged conditions of renumeration and work, and resist change.[22]

The price of professional freedom. The egalitarian argument, at this point, is not just indulging in a crude kind of anti-clericalism directed against the professions in general and medicine in particular. Nor is it necessarily suggesting that professionals are a group of delinquent technicians who should be subjected to political control in the public interest. There are, it is true, overtones of this in the argument. But in the end it recognises the benefits which can flow to society from recognising the professional's right to above-average earnings for work in which he has above-average freedom to exercise his own judgment and organise his own time. This, it believes, can be justified, as long as the professional's right to freedom is not secured at the cost of a loss of basic liberties among the least advantaged members of society, and as long as the least advantaged actually do benefit when the professional is allowed to earn more.[23]

But these conditions, the argument suggests, are not being met. The least advantaged are also the poor and powerless, and there is little sign of their lot improving. In this situation 'the caring professions are in a position to exercise great force in the national and local political areas by adopting clear strategies based on ideologies of equality and justice'.[24] Specifically, these strategies should include policies of positive discrimination which distribute more resources to the poor, both in terms of cash benefits (including family allowances and pensions) and in terms of health, housing and other services. They should also include greater educational and political opportunities for the less advantaged, to give them a greater say in running their own lives.

To achieve these ends, the argument concludes, administrators and professionals should make franker acknowledgment and use of their political role, which is far greater than either pretend. If the professional careers really care, they should, in short, 'stop the buck-passing that serves to protect (their) self-interest'.[25]

Criticism. Criticisms of the egalitarian argument may be made by each of those it criticises, on the grounds that its concern for one set of social facts blinds it to others. To the epidemiologist, and even more the ecologist, these other social facts might include the question whether 'the problem of social incompetence . . . is very largely the problem of mild mental handicap, compounded in turn by the social and educational deprivation occasioned by the slum'.[26] If that is correct, then neither cash benefits nor political opportunities for the poor are enough.

To the clinician, the kind of social facts which the egalitarian argument leaves out of account are, for example 'the urgent character and distracting stresses of hospital work' and the fact 'that doctors like their patients to get better, but do not desert them if things are going badly'.[27] The fact, that is, that professionals have purposes which are more than a matter of self-interest and which they seek, as fallible men and women, to realise in an imperfect world, sometimes seems to escape the 'sociologists' on the sidelines.

From the administrator's point of view too, some facts are absent, and particularly the question of who is going to earn the money to pay for the resources which are to be distributed. It is one thing to condemn inequality and injustice. Like sin, most people are against it. But it is another to balance the budget and provide the incentives which make public expenditure possible. Of course, under the dictatorship of the proletariat, the egalitarian aim might be possible. But the egalitarian argument does not seem willing to see the Western conception of freedom go under, or to buy equality at the expense of liberty.

Do we want equality? This last point raises a further, and more general question about the egalitarian argument. It proposes policies of positive discrimination, which are essentially bureaucratic in character, and also policies of greater participation and self-determination. But it is not clear whether the latter, if implemented, would sustain the former. It is possible, that is, that equality 'does not represent the aspirations of a majority' in British society today, but 'is the aim primarily of an intellectual elite'.[28] And it certainly seems evident, from every society that has ever existed, that some inequalities of power and status are inherent in society's basic and inescapable need to organise itself and order its values.[29]

To these criticisms the egalitarian argument may have no very intellectually respectable reply. Its critics may thus be correct to label it 'sociological', since in one sense it represents a less literate, more numerate, updated version of Charles Dickens. But its roots are older, and the evangelist and perfectionist peer from beneath the sociologist's gown, as he persists:

There never will be a right time for action, never enough resources to eradicate poverty, but the facts exist, and the question the caring professions must face up to one day is quite simple: is poverty of concern to me?[30]

REFERENCES

1. McNeill, W.H. (1976) *Plagues and Peoples*, chapter I, p. 6. Oxford: Basil Blackwell.
2. *op. cit.* chapter VI, p. 260.
3. *op. cit.* p. 291.
4. *ibid.*
5. McKeown, T. (1976) *The Role of Medicine*, chapter 10, p. 170. London: Nuffield Provincial Hospitals Trust.
6. *vide* Brotherston, J. (1976) 'Inequality: Is It Inevitable?' *Equalities and Inequalities in Health*, ed. Carter, C.C. & Peel, J., pp. 73-104. London: Academic Press.
7. *vide* Franklin, A.W. (1976) 'Clinical Medicine', *Medicine in Seventeenth Century England*, ed. Debus, A.G., chapter 6, pp. 118f. Berkeley: University of California Press.

8. Steinfels, P. (1976) 'The Right to Health Care and the Anxiety of Liberalism', *Ethics and Health Policy*, ed. Veatch, R. M. & Branson, R., chapter 10, p. 173. Cambridge, Mass.: Ballinger Publishing Company.
9. *vide* Taylor, T. R. *et al.* (1975) 'Individual Differences in Selecting Patients for Regular Haemodialysis', *British Medical Journal*, 1975, 2, pp. 380-1.
10. *vide* Childress, J. F. (1976) 'Who Shall Live When Not All Can Live?' Veatch & Branson, *op. cit.* chapter 12, pp. 199-212.
11. *vide* Westervelt, F. B. (1976) 'The Selection Process as Viewed from Within' Veatch & Branson, *op. cit.* chapter 13, pp. 213-88.
12. Mackenzie, N. (1971) *The Professional Ethic and the Hospital Service*, chapter 2, p. 9. London: English Universities Press.
13. *vide* Maxwell, R. (1974) *Health Care: The Growing Dilemma*, chapter 4, p. 43. New York: McKinsey & Company Inc.
14. DHSS (1976) *Sharing Resources for Health in England: Report of the Resource Allocation Working Party*. London: H.M.S.O.
    SHHD (1977) *Scottish Health Authorities Revenue Equalization: Report of the Working Party on Revenue Resource Allocation*. Edinburgh: H.M.S.O.
15. Mill, J.S. (1861) *Considerations on Representative Government*, chapter XV (Everyman edition 1910, p. 357. London: J. M. Dent & Sons Ltd.)
16. Bowle, J. (1962) *A New Outline of World History*, chapter V: III, p. 78. London: Allen & Unwin.
17. Bates, P. (1976) 'Poverty and Children', *Contact*, 1976, 2(53), p. 8.
18. Townsend, P. (1974) 'Inequality and the Health Service', *The Lancet*, 15.6.1974, p. 1186.
19. Brotherston, J. (1976) *op. cit.* pp. 73-8.
20. *op. cit.* p. 80.
21. Townsend, P. (1974) *op. cit.* p. 1188.
22. *op. cit.* p. 1189.
23. *vide* Rawls, J. (1972) *A Theory of Justice*. London: Oxford University Press.
24. Bates, P. (1976) *op. cit.* p. 13.
25. *op. cit.* p. 14.
26. Forrest, A. (1976) 'Poverty, Deprivation and Social Incompetence', *Contact*, 1976, 2(53), p. 6.
27. Black, D. (1977) 'Cui bono?' *British Medical Journal*, 1977, 2, p. 1110.
28. Klein, R. (1975) 'Social Policy and the NHS', *British Medical Journal*, 1975, 4, 634-5.
29. Beteille, A. (1977) *Inequality Among Men*, chapter 1. Oxford: Basil Blackwell.
30. Bates, P. (1976) *op. cit.* p. 14.

CHAPTER 5

Professionalism and Politics

IN THE LAST CHAPTER we considered some of the arguments
employed by people with experience of the problem of resource
allocation. Given that their most obvious common characteristic
is the belief of each arguer that his own particular argument is the
most realistic, is there any hope of making the conflict between
them constructive and creative? In this chapter we shall begin by
discussing three ways in which attempts have been and are made
to resolve the conflict: by the appeal, respectively to scientific
measurement, ideological argument, and a definition of health.
Having described and criticised each of these we shall turn,
finally, to consider what may be achieved by the existing professional and political means.

SCIENTIFIC MEASUREMENT

Since the problem of resource allocation is so intractable, and
since so many conflicting answers to it have been suggested, some
professionals and students of health care seek to resolve it by an
appeal to scientific measurement. An approach of this kind has
already been discussed above, in connection with the administrative argument; but it also makes a significant contribution to
other arguments about the right use of resources. In part, the
popularity of this appeal may be attributable to the high status of
science in recent times. But those who adopt this approach,
anxious to do justice to the competing claims and inarticulate
needs of the agents and sufferers involved, may also be acting in
the recollection that justice has to do with impartiality and proportion, and hence with measurement. The consequent collection
of data often is impressive and sometimes is useful. Studies,[1]
for example, showing considerable variation between consultants
in the average duration of hospital treatment for the same condition, suggest clearly enough that justice may not be being done to
someone, be it the patient himself, his family, the potential
patient on the waiting list, or the taxpayer. Or again there is the

question of treatment for ischaemic heart disease at home and in hospital. Measurement by randomised controlled trial has cast doubt on the relative effectiveness of coronary care units;[2] and this in turn has raised the question of the patient's right to be ill in familiar surroundings, especially if these are the most conducive to his recovery. In this case also, of course, the interests of other patients, potential patients and taxpayers are involved; and so again measurement of resources may be suggesting a greater measure of justice in their allocation.

Suggestions, however, are probably the most that can be expected from scientific attempts to deal with the priorities problem. The scientific contribution is limited by at least three factors: the data, their interpretation and their relation to questions of value. The data, for the purposes of determining priorities, have to be available, accurate and reasonably up to date. At present these requirements are rarely all satisfied; and although theoretically this could be remedied, the problems involved are formidable: they involve not only the question of whether the nation could afford the necessary research costs, but also whether professionals would be willing and able to provide sufficiently accurate information in the midst of their other preoccupations. This in turn, of course, assumes that the research workers know what they are looking for, and this raises the question of interpretation. What data, for example, are relevant in what looks like the relatively straightforward case of the divergent consultants? Is it to be judged in terms of costs to the hospital measured by duration of patient stay alone, or should other factors be taken into account, such as consultant-patient and nurse-patient ratios, number of contacts and their costs? Is it necessary further to ask whether earlier discharge shortened waiting times or simply lengthened the time beds were empty? Should the costs of early discharge to the primary care sector also be considered? And how are these costs weighed against the various social costs, to the patient, his family and his employer? The introduction of so indeterminate a notion as social costs in addition to the equally indeterminate notion of health care serves perhaps to show how difficult the interpretation of the data can become.

Clearly, under these circumstances, the student of health care effectiveness and efficiency will want to draw the line somewhere. Other things being equal, he may say, his conclusions stand and raise questions of some practical importance. But if he says this he immediately runs up against the third factor limiting his scientific contribution, its relation to questions of value. In claiming importance for the questions his conclusions raise, he is in practice inviting those who do not share this evaluation to question whether other things really are equal. And in the consequent crosscurrents of conflicting data and whirlpools of ignorance there is some danger either that his original point may sink without trace or that his scientific measurement may begin to seem less like the tool of impartial investigation than the prop of polemic. In the case of the consultants, for example, the possibility of conflict between the values of efficiency and of clinical freedom is obviously present: the research findings cannot settle that. Equally, in the case of coronary care units, the question of where the right to be ill in familiar surroundings should be ranked, in the hierarchy of values health services exist to serve, is not a question empirical research can resolve. Scientific measurement, in short, can and does make useful suggestions about resource allocation. But it cannot measure how useful these suggestions are.

IDEOLOGICAL ARGUMENT

It may, of course, be claimed that science *can* settle these questions, but when this happens the discussion of priorities has taken an ideological turn. Exactly what is meant by the claim that science can settle value questions, can vary: in some cases it is in effect a plea for economist-kings, in others a management ideology, and in others again a species either of Social Darwinism or of Marxism. To term these claims ideological may be simply a form of abuse, but the philosopher's definition of ideology as 'a prescriptive doctrine that is not supported by rational argument' [3] also seems fair. Ideology attempts to argue downwards and outwards in every direction from an original idea or set of ideas. The original idea may in itself be an insight, justifiable up to a point by rational argument, and capable of illuminating many other aspects of the question under discussion. This is certainly true of some perceptions of economists, managers, Social Darwinists and Marxists as far as the health care priorities question is concerned. Problems, however, begin to arise when the insights concerned are set up as ruling ideas.

A contemporary example of such ideological intrusion into the field of health care resources and priorities is Illich's *Medical Nemesis*. Illich has developed insights into the fact that medical treatment can harm as well as heal, into the potential of medical care for creating ever-greater demand, and into the need for individual self-care as well as medical care. He has also, however, developed these insights into an ideology whose ruling idea is that 'the medical establishment has become a major threat to health'. [4] In the process of converting insights into ideology, Illich has marshalled a great deal of evidence and used a number of rational arguments. But not all his arguments are rational: some, for example, depend on the plausibility of such transferred metaphors as 'medical colonisation'[5] (which Imperialists may consider a very good thing); and a certain amount of his evidence is simply wrong, as Professor McKeown[6] has recently demonstrated.

Right or wrong, however, ideology is not simply explanation. It is also prescriptive: its aim, that is, is not just to understand the world but to change it. In the past, some ideologies (Calvinism and Marxism, for example) have achieved this aim, because although unsupported by rational arguments, they were supported by force of arms. This, however, would not have been possible had some of their original insights not been valid and had their descriptions and prescriptions not been, in their time, plausible. Thus it is not surprising to find among the very doctors whom Illich is attacking, those who admit (like school-teachers before them)[7], that 'there is something to what he says'. Nor is it surprising, that when doctors on more mature reflection and careful scrutiny begin to criticise Illich, the suspicion arises that their criticism is primarily a reflection of their professional self-interest.

Interests and purposes. It would be strange if there were not also something to this suspicion, just as, in the past, there was probably something to the *ad hominem* accusations of carnal and bourgeois mindedness which Calvinists and Marxists hurled at their respective opponents. But the point to notice here is how ideology insidiously draws those who engage with it into a defensive posture on ground of the ideology's choosing. In fact, while interests of some kind are always present, self-interest is not the dominant interest of all groups in society: families and religious or other communities, not to mention many hospitals, are examples of this; and it seems probable that this is part of the reason why some professional associations, such as the BMA and the RCN, are unwilling to become simply trade-unions. It is necessary therefore, in the interests of truth, to balance any account of interests with one of purposes.[8] But this is something which, on the whole, ideology is unwilling to do, especially if it regards purposes as the secondary superstructure of an economic, status or other form of self interest. In so far as its critics meet ideology on its own ground therefore, it is difficult for them to criticise it effectively, and their attention is diverted from questions of truth and morality in the matter under discussion.

Perhaps the most serious limitation of ideology then, if sometimes the most difficult to detect, is its tendency to convert the search for truth into an exercise in self-justification. In the field of health care, however, this may be less dangerous than in some others, since the very nature of the subject makes it often extremely difficult to connect the self-interest of individuals and groups with the values they espouse and the purposes they pursue. Doctors, as Illich suggests, do have an interest in staying in business to make a living, but clearly this is not and never has been the only motivation of the majority. And even if it were, it is far from clear that 'medical colonisation' is the easiest or most efficient way of promoting their own interests. A certain difficulty in knowing what is in anyone's interests in fact pervades the whole field of health care and the priorities debate. Is the re-allocation of resources from centres of excellence to deprived areas really in the latter's interest, or does it simply mean that new and cheaper techniques will take longer to develop? If investment in geriatrics and mental disorder entails less for maternity services, will the former areas eventually be any better off? Will higher remuneration for nurses involve closer scrutiny of their role and a consequent reduction in their numbers? And what of the overweight middle-aged politician who decides to invest in coronary care but eventually dies of a less dramatic form of degenerative disease in an overcrowded geriatric ward? Health care is too full of such problems to give self-interest much room for manoeuvre.

Scientific measurement, working from the bottom up, is limited by its data, its interpretation and its relation to questions of value: it can make useful suggestions about resource allocation, but cannot measure how useful these suggestions are. Ideology, working from the top down, is limited by the stubborn refusal of human reality to bend to its categories and by its tendency to distract attention from fundamental questions about what is true and good. Much of the current difficulty in determining health care priorities derives from our society's historical knowledge of these limitations. Aware that scientific measurement alone can only provide very partial clues, we are wary of acting on 'what studies show' until there have been further studies. Aware that ideology embodies the seductive appeal of the half-truth, we are wary of any public discussion of fundamental truths and philosophies, suspecting their respective advocates of self-interest. In the event, particular scientific studies catch the public or professional imagination for a time and become today's fashion. Politics, on the other hand, is left to square off different interests in ways which fuel the suspicion of ideologues, while private conviction looks sadly on and feels rather impotent. The result of all this is something of an *impasse*.

DEFINING HEALTH

Is there any way out of this *impasse*? One possibility, sometimes appealed to, is by defining 'health', deducing appropriate goals for health care from the definition, and in the light of these goals, assigning health care priorities. This is scarcely a project likely to appeal to practical doctors and nurses, but it does seem to have an appeal to planners—or at least that is what a fair amount of writing on the subject suggests. To illustrate this approach and its difficulties, it may be helpful to begin with a recent example.

A WHO example. The World Health Organisation charter's definition of health (as 'a state of complete physical, mental and social well-being') has been much criticised. Conscious of this perhaps, the authors of a recent WHO comparative study of health care attempted to frame a much more sophisticated definition. Health, they suggested,

can be thought of as a responsive functional state where inappropriate responsiveness and maladjustment to change are evidence of an unhealthy state even if scientifically confirmed morbidity and medically defined pathology do not result. It is this dynamic and socially sensitive quality which makes health a mirage; it will vary with the complexity of each macrosystem and with the nature and frequency of deterioration in the ecology that produce equilibrium.[9]

This definition illustrates the difficulty of trying to talk sensibly about health today. The definition in fact is more sensible than it sounds. It rightly says that health is a mirage; and it rightly assumes that if you are going in for bureaucratic health planning on the grand scale, you have to take environmental and social factors into account. As a working definition, devised to give epidemiologists and health planners a framework within which to gather information, its validity can be tested, in one sense at least, by whether it works or not. Are the categories of the embryonic and variously understood science or field of human ecology the right ones? Will it be possible to gather enough information about populations in order to pronounce them healthy before the categories are changed, or the individuals dead and the health care facilities in dust? Only time can tell.

Traditional, medicalised and bureaucratic understandings. In the meantime, however, there is another sense in which the validity of this way of defining health can be questioned. It is understandable why some people should want to define health like this today. The traditional way of understanding health was largely a matter for the individual concerned: unless he was suffering from something which was both painful and out of the ordinary (in his own

91

opinion, or that of his family or peers) or unless he was a wealthy hypochondriac, he was generally considered and considered himself healthy. This understanding, however, has been undermined by medicine's extending awareness of latent disease processes; and because it is now thought to be in danger of being replaced by scientific or medical definitions of statistical normality, many people (especially in an era of expanding activity in the social sciences) want to avert this danger by emphasising the role of environmental and social factors in health. But they also, for very practical reasons, want to measure those factors; and this is why definitions like the one in the WHO study are proposed. The problem about this development, however, is that it does not go far enough. Having delivered the definition of health from the risk of imprisonment within solely scientific and medical terms, it is now in danger of locking it up again in academic and bureaucratic ones.

The problem, in other words, is that while the traditional way of understanding health allowed people to decide for themselves whether or not they were healthy, the new kind of definition leaves little room for this. And while the 'medicalised' or disease definition at least allowed the possibility of the educated patient asking to see his X-rays, or looking up a medical dictionary, the academic-bureaucratic 'inappropriate responsiveness and maladjustment to change' is likely to leave even the educated patient in a state of somewhat Kafkaesque bewilderment. To this, of course, it can immediately be objected that no doctor is intended to employ such criteria in his direct dealings with patients: the point of understanding health in this way is as a working or functional definition, for the use of epidemiologists and planners, who are no more likely to burst into the consulting room than are pathologists. But the difficulty with this objection is that all understandings of health, including the traditional and medicalised versions, are to some extent working or functional definitions. And in the absence of more substantial definitions, working ones tend to fill the vacuum and exercise influence beyond the limited spheres for which they were conceived.

A moral objection. The objection to thinking about health in the way proposed by the WHO study then, is that we may go on thinking of it in this way. The objection is at bottom a moral one, the main thrust of which is perhaps best summed up by quoting four 'theses' propounded by a contemporary sociologist, writing about social planning in general.

Policies for social change are typically made by cliques of politicians and intellectuals with claims to superior insights. These claims are typically spurious.

It is, in principle, impossible to 'raise the consciousness' of anyone, because we are all stumbling around on the same level of consciousness—a pretty dim one.

Every human being knows his own world better than any outsider (including the outsider who makes policy).

Those who are the objects of policy should have the opportunity to participate not only in specific decisions, but in the definition of the situation on which those decisions are based.[10]

If the considerable moral weight of these theses is accepted, it seems unlikely that definitions of health can be of much help in determining priorities. And this is probably what we ought to expect: the essence of 'health' is that it is an unconsidered notion, a common-sense fiction in terms of which people interpret their own physical and mental condition in the absence of painful or sinister signs. If we attempt to say much more than this we enter the realm of the metaphysical or the metaphorical; and while this may yield valid insights, their application to resource allocation involves the risks of ideological prescription which have already been discussed.

PROFESSIONALISM AND POLITICS

The appeal to scientific measurement, to ideological argument and to that version of the latter which seeks to define health, all seem then to offer little hope of resolving the conflict between different arguments about health care goals and priorities. But is there any alternative? Is there in fact any way of making the conflict constructive and creative?

In order to suggest an answer to this question, let us look again at the nature of the current health policy debate. Much of this debate, a recent study has suggested, represents 'a curious blend of the concrete and technical' about how particular financing and administrative techniques should be selected from the range of possibilities, 'and of the abstract and vague' about 'how the services will be provided by the human beings who will be responsible for doing so'.[11] The problem about much recent health policy debate then, as this study puts it, is that it has been concerned with the form rather than the spirit of health care services.[12] But if the question of trust (as we suggested earlier) is the hidden agenda of the debate, the spirit in which care is given is just as crucial as its form. This, of course, may sound like the beginning of another unanswerable metaphysical question. But its practical dimension merits examination.

This was done in the study to which we have just referred, which was based on observation of how doctors in an American group practice organised their work. It assumed that there are basically two ways in which attempts to improve the quality of care can be made: by external bureaucratic forms of control, and by direct mutual professional forms of control in day to day settings. It found, not surprisingly, that bureaucratic controls were highly ineffective where the medical profession was concerned; the doctors studied, valuing their professional freedom, usually found ways of ignoring or subverting them. More disturbingly, however, the study found that professional controls were also weak; and at the level of everyday interaction the doctors were not very successful in influencing the quality of one another's work.

A major reason for the failure of professional controls, the author of the study suggests, was the doctors' fear of bureaucratic control. Any admission that levels of care were less than the best, they seemed to believe, might provoke the imposition of bureaucratic cost or quality controls; and so they refrained from criticism of one another's performance on the ground that no one could adequately judge a colleague's work; they did this moreover despite the fact that they were working as a group rather than as individual practitioners. In doing so, the author suggests, they failed to realise the potential of professionalism for mutual encouragement to better practice; and so they strengthened the case of those who argue for more bureaucratic control.[13]

Bureaucratic control, as the same author points out, is highly inappropriate to health care, which is essentially a discretionary service: this kind of 'worker control' of health services is essentially in the patient's interest, because it alone, at the day to day level, allows 'respect for and attention to the dignity and individuality of each patient seeking help'.[14]

It would of course be a mistake to generalise too freely from a single study, particularly an American one. But it would also be a mistake to assume, even in the British context, that all doctors, and other health care workers for that matter, are equally effective, efficient, imaginative and conscientious in their use of scarce resources or even in their care of patients. No doubt the dangers of bureaucratic forms of cost and quality control can be overstated. But in a situation of conflicting expectations which undermine trust, the possibility of their imposition is real, and the likely effort involved in ignoring or subverting them would be wasteful and distracting.

Potential of professionalism. What this suggests for health care at the everyday level then, is that the problem of allocating scarce resources can be resolved only to the extent to which the potential of professionalism is realised. The nature of professional work means, moreover, that its potential for mutual encouragement to better practice is realised through day to day negotiation between professionals themselves, taking into account the interests and reactions of those they serve. Thus while formal administrative procedures have a part to play in promoting efficiency and effectiveness (as have the proddings of social scientists), the crucial factors are often those of mutual trust and morale. This applies, of course, not only to the work of the traditional professions, but also to that of other skilled occupations in which service to individuals involves an element of discretion or judgment.

While there is clearly no general method for realising the potential of professionalism, a major obstacle to this at present would seem to be a fashionable lack of confidence in professionalism itself. This is reflected in defensiveness among the professionals and, among their critics, in the belief that there exists some (as yet unspecified) viable alternative to discretionary worker control in health care. Perhaps the first step towards removing this obstacle then, is by disabusing ourselves of the illusory alternative.

The problem of allocating scarce resources cannot of course simply be tackled at the day to day level, since public provision of health care services inevitably involves the necessity for larger scale public decisions. But here too the shape of the problem is strikingly similar. The form of the service, the conditions under which health workers' services are provided and the range of services offered to different sections of the population, were all traditionally determined by the market, albeit tempered by charity, and in the case of public health by public provision. Today, with much more general public provision, the medium is politics. The problem, however, is again one of lack of confidence, in this case lack of confidence in politics.

Potential of politics. Lack of confidence in politics is understandable, and particularly as a way of allocating scarce resources in health care. Self-interest and cynical manipulation often seem to flourish in the political arena, and rationality appears overcome by ideology and rhetoric. It is not surprising therefore that some people wish to keep politics out of health, just as others wish to keep it out of education, defence, or industry. But the pervasiveness of politics in an increasingly affluent and well-educated modern society is not easily dissipated; and the reduction of those unattractive features which breed lack of confidence in politics is more likely to be achieved through better political activity than through less.

To say this is not to defend the beliefs, programmes or practices of any particular political party or group, since politics itself is based on the recognition that different interests exist within any community. In practice, politics is the attempt to give each of these interests 'a share in power in proportion to their importance to the welfare and survival of the community'.[15] Since the different interests will frequently differ in their estimation of their own and others' respective importance, politics of course will remain a matter of barely contained conflict, and open to abuse. Nevertheless, the dangers of political inaction are in the end greater than those of political activity; and one of the commonest causes of politics' unattractive features is the failure of those who criticise them to become involved in politics, accepting its limitations, mastering its complexities and attempting to refine its methods. The ultimate danger from this quarter is the suppression of politics itself, as different interests within society sacrifice (or are compelled to sacrifice) their share in power under some form of dictatorship or totalitarianism; and here, while the possibility of abuse remains, that of redress is severely reduced.

Politics, however, is not just a necessary evil but also a potential good. Based on a recognition of the rights and responsibilities of different interests within the community, it can be a binding as well as a divisive force; and to the extent that it is open and honest, politics can provide creative and constructive ways of recognising restraints, increasing trust and resolving problems. Clearly a major obstacle to realising this potential, as in the case of professionalism, is the belief that there exists some better way of ordering society, determining its priorities and allocating its resources. But unless, in the sphere of health care, the majority wish to return to the market, or unless different groups within the community are willing to sacrifice their share in power (neither of which seem likely) there is no alternative to politics as a way of settling the larger questions of health care resources and priorities. Again, therefore, disabusing ourselves of an illusory but unspecified alternative would seem to be the first step towards realising the potential of the best method to hand.

The problems of resource allocation in health care then can ultimately be resolved only by the exercise in appropriate contexts of professional or political judgment, co-operatively and on the basis of limited information. Some of the most difficult problems of course are those in which the context does not make clear which of these forms of judgment is appropriate. But these problems are even less likely to be resolved if the potential of professionalism and of politics is unrealised through lack of confidence;

and as long as the exercise of either kind of judgment is avoided, in the illusory hope of science or ideology providing a better solution, the problem can only get worse.

REFERENCES

1. Cooper, M.H. (1975) *Rationing Health Care*, p. 56. London: Croom Helm.
2. Cochrane, A.L. (1972) *Effectiveness and Efficiency*, pp. 50-4. London: Nuffield Provincial Hospitals Trust.
3. Raphael, D.D. (1976) *Problems of Political Philosophy*, p. 17. London: Macmillan.
4. Illich, I. (1975) *Medical Nemesis*, p. 11. London: Calder and Boyars.
5. *ibid.*
6. McKeown, T. (1976) *The Role of Medicine*, pp. 166-71. London: Nuffield Provincial Hospitals Trust.
7. *vide* Illich, I. (1973) *Deschooling Society*. Harmondsworth, Penguin.
8. *vide* Raphael (1976) *op. cit.* p. 38.
9. Kohn, R., White, K.L. (1976) *Health Care: An International Study*, chapter 5, p. 58. London: Oxford University Press.
10. Berger, P. (1974) *Pyramids of Sacrifice: Political Ethics and Social Change*, p. 13. London: Allen Lane.
11. Freidson, E. (1975) *Doctoring Together: A Study of Professional Social Control*, Part I, chapter 1, p. 5.
12. *op. cit.* Part IV, chapter 15, p. 256.
13. *op. cit.* p. 246.
14. *op. cit.* p. 254.
15. *vide* Crick, B. (1964) *In Defence of Politics*. Harmondsworth: Penguin.

APPENDIXES

MEASUREMENT: HEALTH ECONOMICS
Models, Achievements and Limitations

IN HIS FOREWORD to the collected papers of one of the first health economics meetings in this country, Professor Alan Williams writes:

The role of economics in the medical care system is understandably a matter of some controversy. It generates a suspicion that ruthless, profit-seeking tycoons will be turned loose in a field in which it is rightly felt that humanitarian considerations should predominate. It is also seen as a potential threat to 'clinical freedom', to the notion that the practitioner's duty is to provide the best possible medical care for his patient, regardless of who the patient is and no matter what the cost (Williams, A.H., 1972).

At another conference in the same year (1970) the American health economist Rashi Fein pointed out:

The general attractiveness of economic arguments has, at least in part, derived from the belief that economics is value-free, neutral and objective. Thus, economic arguments relying on the hard criteria of the market, on 'profit' and on 'loss' carried a special weight (a weight that was, perhaps, increased by the fact that economists use data, jargon, and methodology that are somewhat mysterious to the uninitiated). The special attractiveness of economic arguments in social areas (for example in the case of programmes that deal directly with people) is increased by the fact that these fields generally lack rigorous monetary guidelines for decision-making. (Fein, R., 1971).

The purpose of this paper is to present some of the models that economists have developed and applied to the field of resource allocation in health care, and to argue that these still require considerable development and clarification before the public, the government, civil service, health boards or doctors put too much trust or hope in them. I shall argue that health economists are in danger of over selling descriptive, analytical or even predictive techniques and models, and that they have not given due regard to dispelling the myths of measurability and of being value-free.

Certainly economists do use jargon, but it is difficult for all disciplines which attempt to be specific to avoid this particular pitfall. However, jargon may make interpretation of the values and assumptions difficult for the non-economist to identify and criticise. Feldstein's examination of hospital costs is one example:

Although doctors at present appear to show little interest in cost when choosing between inpatient and outpatient care for a particular patient, to the extent that they do consider costs, their attention focuses on average rather than marginal costs. If the simple fact that long-run marginal cost per case is substantially less than average cost per case were properly appreciated by doctors and hospital administrators, admission rates and the intensity of use of hospital capacity might be substantially higher (Feldstein, M.S., 1967).

Such an analysis shifts our attention away from considering family and community costs, and also from considering the possibility that an increase in community resources might remove the need to admit patients to hospital at all.

The sight of a title like 'Revealed Preferences and the Value of a Life' (Jones-Lee, M.W., 1973) may on the other hand send shivers down the spines of doctors and patients even when not fully understood. Furthermore, the use of a 'mysterious' methodology may often produce conclusions which are understandable, but which may not be quite as reliable as they first appear. For example, in 1972 Piachaud and Weddell reported that:

The results at three years after treatment show no difference between the two methods of treatment. The estimates of cost to the Health Service and the community are greater for surgical treatment than injection compression sclerotherapy. On the basis of these results it would benefit the patient, the health service and the community, if the majority of patients were treated in out-patients by injection compression sclerotherapy (Piachaud, D. & Weddell, J.M., 1972).

More recently, however, evidence has been produced that after a longer time period the clinical outcome was less satisfactory than that found by Piachaud and Weddell (*BMJ* 1975).

Other conclusions may, like the Jones-Lee title, stimulate an immediate sense of inhumanity:

The cost-benefit analysis of long term maintenance haemodialysis indicates that there is a gulf between the cost of the service and economic benefit. The difference may be considered to represent one estimate of the price society is prepared to pay to maintain life. Using 'best estimates' from available data we found that the implicit social value of maintaining a patient on haemodialysis to be approximately £4720 per annum in hospital or £2600 at home. The analysis would suggest that society must look carefully at alternative uses for health expenditure before extending indiscriminately to large sections of the population these treatment programmes or others similarly expensive (Buxton, M.J. & West, R.R., 1975).

This kind of approach is not in fact new. In 1667 Sir William Petty estimated that during outbreaks of the plague every pound expended on transporting people outside of London and caring for them for three months, yielded a return of £84; and he went on to argue that better medicine, which was to be assured by state intervention, could save the lives of 200,000 subjects a year. This, when valued at the lowest price of slaves (£20), was a large sum (Fein, R., 1971).

This concept of the economic value of man reappears throughout the writings of the early reformers like Edwin Chadwick, and it is not surprising that health economists have been shunned by the medical profession. Attempts to value life (or health) are nigh on committing the cardinal sin of placing the economist in a god-like role.

Like it or not however, in a world of finite resources, of 'ill health', and of the technical ability of groups of doctors to keep spending money on saving more lives or increasing the stock of the nation's health, or in carrying out research, there is an *implicit* valuation of life (and even of *a* life) at every stage of medical care provision. This is not a myth but a fact of life which unfortunately is often surrounded by medical and economic mystery, and sometimes, by medical myth. In fact although it is the task of this paper to identify certain myths in health economics, it must be said that this subject itself is largely to be held responsible for revealing the myth that life and health cannot be valued. It can and is, but nearly always implicitly.

In an address to a meeting at the Scottish Health Service Centre in February 1976, G. Mooney was at particular pains to make this point:

Within existing decision making, a decision to implement some policy at a cost of £x implies that the benefits are valued at £x at least (otherwise it would not have been implemented). On the other hand, a decision not to implement some policy costing £y implies that the benefits of such implementation are less than £y (otherwise it would have been implemented). What cost-benefit analysis seeks to do is to make explicit these

H   103

implied values and judgments and thereby rationalise and improve decision making (Mooney, G., 1976).

The crucial questions would therefore seem to be (1) how accurate and reliable are these attempts to make explicit the implied values and judgments of decision making, and (2) what value judgments do economists make when evaluating health services?

If we look back at the development of economic expertise in the running of the National Health Service, we may note that there was no formal commitment on the part of the Department of Health and Social Security (or the Ministry of Health) until 1970. The increasing costs of the National Health Service had prompted the Guillebaud Report of 1956, and the pharmaceutical manufacturers established the Office of Health Economics in 1962 'because of their concern at that time over the widespread misunderstandings about expenditure on health (Teeling-Smith, G.E., 1972), but it also seems that economists themselves were fairly reluctant to enter the medical care world, in an establishment sense, for Cohen observed that:

It was necessary (for the Ministry of Health and later the DHSS) first to identify and cultivate those, beside the few pioneers, who might have a contribution to make . . . (economists proved the shyest birds; the example of Feldstein had not been followed and it was not until early 1970 that it was possible to arrange a conference under Professor Alan Williams, University of York, to discuss what part they might usefully play) (Cohen, R.H.L., 1971).

In fact, of course, economists had been researching the health care services for some time before 1970, but there is the danger that myths may begin to develop often as the result of wishful thinking on the part of the laity rather than of deliberate power policies by the practitioners. At that 1970 conference in York both the men from the Department and the health economists themselves were at some pains to state the difficulties and limitations inherent in health economics, for example:

The Select Committee on Procedure has strongly advocated the development of output budgeting by Government departments and envisages that this would ultimately be the basis for parliamentary discussion of priorities.

We are very conscious on the health and welfare side of the Department that in this new approach to judging priorities, we may well lose in the struggle for the proper share of the national cake if we are not able to present our case more scientifically than we do now.

We think that the dangers for us are, firstly, that with new techniques of economic appraisal, a greater share of public expenditure may go to those sections which can show clearly an economic return on investment, and that an unconscious bias may develop towards favouring an economic rather than a social programme. For example, a nationalised industry may be able to show a profit return on capital investment whereas at present we cannot demonstrate any comparable return from capital devoted to hospital building. Secondly, we fear that, even within the social programmes, health and welfare will suffer by comparison, for example, with education and roads because we cannot yet express our needs in mathematical terms nor show that better returns will come from increases in health and welfare expenditure as compared with increases in other outlets for public spending.

This presents us with a dilemma. We ought not to introduce new economic techniques just to be fashionable. We ought not to ask economists to use their scarce skills in producing economic measurements of the health and welfare services if the end result is likely to be highly artificial. But if we cannot find meaningful measurements of input and output we may be forced to go for the best that we can devise, even though they may be somewhat artificial, simply in order to avoid being left behind in the struggle for our share of the national cake (Salter, H.C., 1972).

As if in confirmation of the doubts inherent in Mr Salter's paper, Professor Williams concludes his foreword to the collection of papers from the 1970 York conference with the following:

The fact of the matter is that all of the work reported here is of a pioneering nature. The authors would be the first to recognise the limitations of their collective contributions and no one is yet in a position to assert that we know the right way to tackle any of the problems, still less that we have come up with any definitive answers. But when exploring unknown territory, patient probing on many points is frequently a rewarding strategy, and it is to be hoped that it proves so in the economics of medical care (Williams, A.H., 1972).

Since 1970 when, apart from the York conference, the first two professional economists were appointed to the Department of Health and Social Security in London, both the number of economists working on health care and the quantity of published work has increased considerably. Two research meetings of interest to economists throughout the UK are held each year, there is an annual bibliographic review giving extracts from publications and work in progress, and there are now (February

1976) eight health economists at the DHSS. Although authorship of the consultative document 'Priorities for Health and Personal Social Services in England' (DHSS 1976a) was not disclosed, it is very apparent that the Department's economists played a considerable part in its formulation, and the senior economic advisor was a DHSS member of the Resource Allocation Working Party (DHSS 1976b) and three others were members of subgroups.

Without subjecting my theory to any rigorous analysis, it is my contention that although there has been an increase in the quality of the data collected and more realistic models in which to fit this data, there is a danger that health economists are beginning to believe that their techniques and numbers are reliable, and unbiased, and that the public may fall for their 'scientific authenticity' without giving them due criticism. It *may* therefore be no bad thing that implementation of proposals takes time, though this in itself may be cost-ineffective. As I said earlier, my argument is that economists are in danger of over-selling their techniques at a time when these may not be sufficiently reliable, or the costs of reliability may be greater than the benefits. This is not to say, however, that I feel that health economics is not worth doing. Although I would not subscribe to the view of Culyer, who writes: '(This book) has been written in the firm belief that there exists no other framework of thought (other than that of the economist) that can at the same time both provide a relevant and thoroughly worked out corpus of analysis through which the problems (sometimes agonising ones) posed by alternative choices can be elucidated . . .' (Culyer, A.J., 1976), I do believe that economists have contributed and should continue to contribute to the lively debate surrounding the allocation of scarce resources to health and social welfare services. Rather like the development of sophisticated clinical equipment, economics and economic techniques should be selectively developed and each proposal adopted only when the technique behind the proposal is shown to be valuable.

There is however a second and perhaps more insidious problem. The concentration of health economic research into 'policy research' may restrict the amount of more general questioning into the values underpinning the NHS and the role of medicine and doctors in an industrial society like Britain today (Rex, J., 1974; Illich, I., 1976; McKeown, T., 1976; Navarro, V., 1976). By and large economists today have only entered this debate through the larger debate about economic growth (Mishan, J., 1977). Such comments that come from health economists have been generally flippant 'the arcadian remedies implicit in Illich's diagnosis of "structural iatrogenesis" (iatrogenic disease is that induced by medical practice) are neither generally desired in modern societies nor would they seem particularly desirable' (Culyer, A.J., 1976), and the only positive contribution to the debate seems to have come from Peter Draper and his colleagues at Guy's (Draper, P. *et al.*, 1976).

It is impossible in a paper like this to review the vast literature produced by health economists. (For attempts to do this, see the annual bibliography produced by the SSRC Health Economists Group; Weissbrod, B.A., 1975; Williams, A.H., 1975.) Instead, the paper is divided into two parts, the first of which selects some studies of resource allocation for particular diseases, patient groups or clinical techniques. The second section deals with more general problems of resource allocation, allocation between different patient groups or clinical programmes. Obviously the two are closely interlinked and should not really be dealt with separately, but such a breakdown makes for ease of presentation and comprehension. In both sections, I shall try and deal with the questions raised about the measurability myth and the value-free myth.

INVERSE-PROGRAMMING AND COST-BENEFIT ANALYSIS
Two of the techniques which have been developed in the main body of applied economics and adapted to investigate practical problems of resource allocation within the NHS are inverse-programming, and cost-benefit analysis.

Let us begin with a very simplified example of the resource allocation problem facing any administrator whose current problem is the management of existing resources (i.e. non-capital expenditure) and who has only a marginal increment in his annual budget and little chance of major reallocation of resources between services.

Consider the hypothetical case of a maternity service providing only two types of care for low-risk expectant mothers from a particular community (Hawgood, J. & Morley, R., 1969; Porter, A.M.D., 1971; Lavers, R.J., 1972; Morley, R., 1972;). A hospital provides 'early discharge' and 'normal stay' care and this is the only choice there is. The hospital is equipped with nine beds (which we will approximate to 3200 bed-days per year) and is staffed by two doctors working 4800 hours per year, and five midwives working 10,000 hours per year.

It is known that, on average, each 'early discharge' case requires two bed-days, six doctor hours, and ten midwife hours of
107

the total available resources. Similarly, each 'normal stay' case requires eight bed-days, four doctor-hours and twenty midwife-hours. (These figures are not in the least supposed to represent current practice in a real hospital.)

This information is enough to determine the hospital's technology, and to ensure technical efficiency. Table 1 summarises this information, and Table 2 solves the three equations on the assumption that the maximum amount of each resource is available. Thus, if all 4800 doctor-hours are devoted to normal stay cases, 1200 mothers can be cared for, whereas if they were devoted solely to early-discharge cases, then only 800 mothers could be cared for. Figure 1 translates this information into graphic form—the three solid lines joining the two axes representing the technically feasible number of cases for each resource. Any point on or within the boundary OABDE is technically feasible given the constraints of each resource line, and any point on ABDE is technically efficient. Any point to the left and below ABDE (e.g. F)

TABLE 1		TABLE 2
Doctor Hours	$4N + 6E \leq 4800$	N = 1200, E = 800
Midwife Hours	$20N + 10E \leq 10000$	N = 500, E = 1000
Bed Days	$8N + 2E \leq 3200$	N = 400, E = 1600

N: Normal Stay Care; E: Early Discharge Care

FIGURE 1

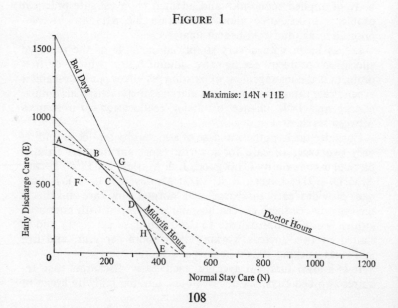

Maximise: $14N + 11E$

108

is technically inefficient as more of both types of care can be provided without change in the technology or in the total amount of available resources. A point to the right and above ABDE (e.g. G) is impossible given the present technology and resource availability. It will be observed, however, that only a shortage of midwives prevents point G from being technically feasible.

Without any knowledge of patients' preferences or of doctors' evaluation of the benefits of the two activities, the maternity hospital would be providing care efficiently if the level of care corresponded to any point on ABDE. Suppose, however, that the hospital is operating in a free-market situation and that patients are willing to pay up to, but not more than, £11 for 'early-discharge' care and £14 for 'normal-stay' care—in other words these prices represent the patients' evaluations of the benefit that they will derive from the two kinds of care—then the hospital is in a position to plan supply of the two types of care so that the blend of output maximises total consumer benefit. The prices that mothers have put on the two types of care reveal that an additional 'normal-stay' case is $\frac{14}{11} = 1·27$ times more worthwhile (beneficial) than an additional 'early-discharge' case. Diagrammatically, this benefit function (more generally referred to as 'the objective function') is represented by any line with the slope $-\frac{14}{11}(-1·27)$, and the maximum blend of output is achieved by moving this line away from the origin until it is tangential to ABDE. At this point, total benefit will be at a maximum. From Figure 1 it can be observed that maximum benefit is achieved when output is at point B where care is provided to 150 'normal-stay' cases and 700 'early-discharge' cases. It will be seen that at this blend of output, the total quantity of both doctor-hours and midwife-hours are used up, whilst some bed-days are lying idle.

Now, suppose that the patients' preferences change so that they are willing to pay up to £33 for 'normal-stay' care, but still no more than £11 for 'early discharge' care. Such a change in preferences alters the slope of the benefit function from $-1·27$ to $-3·00$. If the hospital's administrators are aware of this change, they will reallocate their available resources in such a way that the blend of output maximises the new benefit function. If the blend of output continued to be point B, then the total benefit would be £12,650, whereas if the blend was where the new benefit function was tangential to ABDE, point D, then total benefit would be equivalent to £14,300. At this blend of output, bed-days and midwife-hours constrain further provision, whilst doctor-hours are slack.

The purpose of this simple example is to show that the planning of an economically efficient supply of maternity services is, in the short-run, dependent upon the prior knowledge of three sets of information.

First, it must be possible to describe and measure the technology of the production process. This involves being able to define what is being produced (the outputs) and then being able to measure the amount of each resource (input) that is required to produce one unit of output. Secondly, the total quantity available of each resource input must be known. Thirdly, consumers' preferences for each unit of output must be known.

In theory all these sets of information are required if economic efficiency is to be achieved. How realistically can the economist help the health service planner? Leaving aside the problem of validating certain mathematical assumptions—in particular the linearity of the production functions—there are a number of major practical difficulties:

First of all, how is output defined? Traditionally, output has been defined and measured by using through-put, for example the number of hospital discharges (and deaths) and the number of episodes of illness in general practice. In the case of our simple example, the birth of a live child is a very definite through-put, but is nearer to output than many other disease-type 'through-puts' that are used as output measurements. More recently, health economists have argued for more 'health type' definitions by using 'health indicators' which involve the measurement of the number of people in certain categories measured in terms of disability and pain over time and for intensity (Culyer, A. J. *et al.*, 1971; Grogono, A. W. & Woodgate, D. J., 1971; Rosser, R. & Watts, V., 1972; Williams, A. H., 1974a).

Secondly, once the measure of output has been defined, the economist has to be able to measure the amount of each resource input that is required to produce one unit of output. This is a complex and time consuming enough task when dealing with through-put, and one that is particularly complicated by the fact that it is often exceptionally difficult to separate the amount spent on one output from another. Moreover, substitutability between inputs in the production of one unit of output may in itself mean considerable effort in terms of research and evaluation. When health indicators are employed as the measure of output, it is now necessary to mount another research project to measure the amount of each resource that is required to obtain a particular state of ability and pain-reduction over time.

Thirdly, without any prices to indicate consumer preferences, how are the values that go on the objective function derived?

Inverse programming is a technique which allows the implicit values currently put on the objective function to be extrapolated, but there is no simple way of deriving the values that *ought* to be on the objective function for *future* planning decisions. As far as inverse programming goes, all one can say is 'These seem to be the values that planners are putting on the outputs at present, is this really what you think they are, or should be?' For example, in a study of the Sunderland maternity services, ten mutually exclusive activities (or outputs) were defined. Table 3 gives details of the actual levels of provision (output) which in this case were measured as throughputs and the implied values that health service administrators were putting on these activities. Thus, for example, they were valuing home confinements (DCC) more highly than 48-hour stay in hospital. Although the model could then be used to determine which resources should be increased or cut-back (and by how much) if one wanted to change these values, it in no way provided a predictive tool in terms of the ideal levels of provision of home confinements compared to 48-hour stay. Moreover, as we have already noted, output of the

TABLE 3

| | | | HANI | | | | | | | |
	DANC	HANO	1	2	3	DCC	HEDC	HNSC	HLSC	HPNI
Actual provision	11234	20893	363	43	84	1330	351	2313	119	21
Implied weights	0·02	0·02	0·3	0·7	0·7	1·4	1·0	1·4	1·8	0·9

HEDC = 1

DANC   Domiciliary Antenatal care measured as the total number of antenatal visits and attendances at clinics.

HANO   Hospital Antenatal care (outpatients) measured by the total number of attendances at Sunderland Maternity Hospital.

HANI 1, HANI 2, HANI 3. Hospital Antenatal care (inpatients) measured by the number of cases discharged from the hospital wards with different lengths of stay.

DCC   Domiciliary Confinement care measured by the total number of cases delivered at home.

HEDC   Hospital Early-discharge care measured by the total number of cases discharged after 48-hour stay.

HNSC   Hospital Normal-stay care measured as the number of mothers discharged from hospital between 3rd and 10th day, with an average length of stay of 8·0 days.

HLSC   Hospital Long-stay care measured as the number of cases requiring stays in hospital of more than 10 days. Average length of stay was 12·3 days.

HPNI   Hospital Postnatal care (inpatients) measured as the number of women discharged after admission to hospital for specialist post-delivery care. Average length of stay 8·0 days.

various activities is measured in terms of through-put rather than health, the data to derive the technical co-efficients (the relationships between inputs and outputs) were derived from retrospective hospital records rather than prospective, and no attempt was made to establish that each production function was technically efficient. Moreover, although data were collected on domiciliary nursing and midwifery resources, GP resources were not included in the model because of the complexity of measurement. In other words, the potential areas of unreliability in this type of model were so great as to limit its use to that of a discussion model rather than as a realistic planning model, and this was in the relatively simple field of maternity care.

The second technique that should be discussed is that of *cost-benefit analysis*, which

rests on the proposition that we should provide services only if their benefits outweigh their costs. In subscribing to that view however, we (perhaps unwittingly) commit ourselves to the following set of propositions:

  (i) It is possible to separate one service from another service in a sensible way.
 (ii) There is a possibility of a choice between them.
(iii) It is possible to estimate the outcome associated with each alternative service.
 (iv) It is possible to value these outcomes.
  (v) It is possible to estimate the cost of providing each service.
 (vi) That these costs and benefits can be weighed against each other.
(vii) We should cease providing those services, the costs of which outweigh the benefits. (Williams, A.H., 1974b)

As with the inverse-programming model just described, the principles behind cost-benefit analysis do in fact provide a very useful framework for thinking about the problems of resource allocation. (For example, Klarman, H.E., 1965; Klarman, H.E. *et al.*, 1968; Brooks, R., 1971; Pole, J.D., 1972; Piachaud, B. & Weddell, J.M., 1972; Reynell, R.C. & Reynell, M.C., 1972; Wager, R., 1972; Davies, G.M., 1973; Glass, N.J. & Russell, I.T., 1974; Buxton, M.J. & West, R.R., 1975; Carter, F. *et al.*, 1976; Rich, G. *et al.*, 1976).

In particular, cost-benefit analysis (and its companion technique cost-effectiveness) forces decision makers to consider not only the costs and benefits which accrue to the sponsoring body, but also the spill-over (externality) effects in terms of benefits and costs to other providers of health care services, to other groups of patients and to society in general. Similarly, the concept of opportunity costs (the fact that by gaining benefits from investing in one particular area one sacrifices benefits in another alternative area) forces decision makers to think in terms of alternatives and the relative values of these alternatives.

However, it is apparent from Williams' statement that many of the problems associated with linear-programming are pertinent to the cost-benefit approach. For example, there may be considerable difficulty in distinguishing one service (output) from another and, as already pointed out, this may cause problems in terms of relating the quantity of inputs required to one unit of output. The question of estimating outcomes associated with each service and the valuation of these outcomes is similar to the problem of defining health and health indicators, and the derivation of consumer preferences. Furthermore, it should be pointed out that the market prices are only valid as estimates of costs if one assumes that the present distribution of income and wealth in the country is acceptable.

In the conclusion to his paper, Williams asks the question: 'Is it all too difficult?' and he points out that the answer to the question, 'do the benefits of a certain action outweigh the costs?', proves to be a very difficult problem even to formulate satisfactorily, and attempting to answer it demands considerable commitment to one's task. He continues:

The trouble with the more comfortable ways (muddling through) is that they foster the illusion that, if cost-benefit analysis is not done, the issues which it poses can be avoided, whereas the reality is that these issues are all still present and they all still have to be resolved. If health services planning is not to be based on the principle that unwitting decisions are likely to be better than witting decisions then the cost-benefit approach must become a part of every decision maker's intellectual equipment (Williams, A. H., 1974).

A similar sentiment is to be found in Culyer, A.J. (1976) after his review of cost-benefit studies.

I would agree with Williams that the cost-benefit approach should be a part of every decision maker's intellectual equipment, and I also feel that the concepts and ideas used by health economists are valuable to both doctors and planners. What seems slightly disturbing, however, is that most of the difficulties and the problems that are being investigated are related to the technical ones from the economic end—the reliability of the actual technical model, particularly as a predictive tool. My point here is that all too often health economists seem to assume that although the data are difficult to obtain, they can be got and measurement is possible, so that the technical problems are the ones which should occupy more of their time and energy.

Difficulties also arise because, often, we know relatively little about the production process whereby final outputs are created. I do not ignore the difficulties involved in creating data and reporting systems to measure the achievements of limited and well-defined goals (for example reduction in incidence of a particular disease). In no small measure our relative ignorance about many health matters relates to the fact that our data systems are underdeveloped and—in terms of funds and personnel—undernourished. Far too often we simply do not have the data we need for analytical purposes. These difficulties, however, are surmountable and better reporting and data systems can be created. I refer instead to even greater problems associated with the measurement of outputs which are amorphous in concept, outputs such as 'higher levels of health' and which are contributed to by many factors (for example, housing, income, nutrition, environment, medical care of all kinds), factors whose relative contribution may differ for different persons and whose relative contribution is largely unknown (Fein, R., 1971).

I hope it is clear from my discussion about inverse-programming and cost-benefit analysis that I agree about the conceptual problems of measuring health. I do not unfortunately agree about the surmountability of data-collection problems; in fact, I would come closer to C. Wright Mills' suggestion that we are being snowed under by data that we don't know how to cope with, and for which we do not know the explanations (Mills, C.W., 1959). And whilst Culyer has argued that 'attaching an explicit value to a unit gain in a health index has every prospect of leading to a much more humanitarian and egalitarian NHS' (Culyer, 1976), the potential for developing record linkage and constructing disease registers may well conflict with other societal values that people hold precious.

Furthermore, the development of prospective recording systems which are able to measure changes in health status and the required resource inputs must inevitably involve doctors, nurses and other health personnel in more record-keeping and it is my impression that increasing demands for data collection are likely to lead to hostility and a decreasing return in accuracy. Fortunately, there do seem to be other economists who at least recognise the problem:

The effect of different treatments on health status is partly measured on the cost side through savings in patient time. It is however necessary to have a separate measure of the health output of different treatments. As such, an adaptation of the 'York Health Status Index' will be used (Culyer, A.J. *et al.*, 1971).

This index has intensity and duration as main concepts very well suited to describe the symptoms of patients with gall-stones. The construction of the index will start with an ordinal ranking of different possible health status for patients with gall-stones during and after treatment. As the project is still in a very early stage no definite description and ranking of different status has yet been done. To receive (derive) a health status index for the whole period the different statuses have to be given weights. There are a lot of problems in assigning these weights. If we say that it is fifteen times worse to be in status A than in status B, does this mean that it is equal to be one day in status A and fifteen days in status B. Can we be sure that the same index will give histories between which the patient is indifferent? Or do we also have preferences over different 'profiles' over time?

The York Health Status Index can be described as

$$Y = \int_0^n I(t)e^{-it}dt, \quad \text{where} \quad I(t) = S(t)P_S + R(t)P_R$$

and a more formal formulation is

$$Y = \int_0^n ((S(t)P_S(t, S_0^t) + R(t)P_R(t, R_0^t))e^{-it}dt.$$

where Y = York Health Index
       I = Health Status (intensity)
       S = Pain
       R = Restriction of activity
       i = discount rate
       P = prices

which allow the valuation to vary over time apart from discounting. *However to feed this index with information is a heroic task* (Jonsson B., 1976).

Another difficulty is that the collection of data for a particular cost-benefit or linear-programming model takes considerable time. In some situations the medical technology relevant to the alternative forms of treatments change during this time, and this may of course mean that one's results are out-of-date even before writing up (Mills, M., 1976).

One other particularly important (but unpredictable) effect of time on outcome effectiveness is provided by the example, already cited, of the treatment of varicose veins.

As far as values are concerned, inverse-programming may, with careful collection of data, reveal the values at present put on the objective function by health service planners but it certainly has no claim as a predictive tool, and the problems of carrying out market research into public opinion or of asking doctors are obvious.

At a slightly different level, Glass has pointed out that Piachaud and Weddell were particularly fortunate in that their clinical outcomes were similar for both types of treatment they considered, and that therefore it was a simple matter of saying that one should choose the least costly of the two equally effective procedures. As he points out: 'This enables them to skirt round the (more interesting) problem where the less costly method also turns out to be significantly less clinically effective' (Glass, N.J., 1973).

Taking this one stage further, all cost-benefit analyses of health care services have dealt with the application of alternative forms of treatment for rather discreet clinical conditions. Thus, for example, one cost-benefit analysis shows that treatment B is more beneficial and costs less than treatment A in, for example, the treatment of gall-stones; another cost-benefit analysis may show that in the treatment of patients suffering from varicose veins, treatment C is preferable to treatment D. No one has yet tried to answer the question, if we can only pursue one of these two forms of treatment, i.e. only treat gall-stones or varicose veins, which one do we choose? Or, how do we compare treatment C with treatment B?

MORE GENERAL PROBLEMS

The technique that has come closest to attempting to evaluate outcomes between different disease categories has been programme budgeting (nothing to do with linear programming) and it may be worth noting that the Scottish Home and Health Department is continuing to fund the Health Economics Research Unit at Aberdeen University for a further five years with a view to developing both programme budgeting and cost-benefit analysis.

A. *Programme budgeting.* Programme budgeting originated in the United States and only came to the National Health Service in Britain with the appointment of economists to the Department of Health and Social Security in 1970. The senior of these advisers, J.D.Pole, who has recently summarised the history of planning and accounting in the NHS, has observed that:

The philosophy of programme budgeting (PPB) as it was developed in the United States was based on the assumed tendency for the activities of bureaucracies to acquire a momentum of their own, and progressively to lose their orientation towards the objects they were instituted to pursue. . . . The essential aim of PPB was to specify programmes each of which should contribute to some well-defined objective, with the view to comparing their costs and effectiveness. Only by identifying objectives would it be possible to make sense of the activities of the organisation, while in order to evaluate these activities they must be organised into programmes (Pole, J.D., 1974).

Pole in fact admits that there are major complications of apportionment and definition involved in programme budgeting, and he also notes that its usefulness is limited to an account of expenditure by output orientated categories (e.g. mental illness, disability, maternity, etc.) and that we have no knowledge of the effectiveness of each activity within a programme, nor do we know the contribution of particular inputs to particular outputs.

By 1974 the Department of Health was committed to programme budgeting and had hired more economists who were, as Pole's article reveals, very aware of the difficulties that were involved in their task. The first document to reflect the skills of these economists was the Department of Health's *Priorities for Health and Personal Social Services in England* (DHSS, 1976a).

I cannot include the Scottish document (SHHD, 1976). This seems to have been a little more circumspect in that, whilst adopting similar programme headings, it does not attempt the sophistication of the English document, and thereby seems to have been spared the attack that greeted the latter. Even so Professor Jennett (Jennett, B., 1976) has argued that although general practice is getting an increased share of the budget, this has not been calculated on the basis of rational analysis like cost-benefit or cost-effectiveness (techniques which have been most commonly carried out in hospital) but on value-judgments about the efficiency of health centres and community teams.

A (i). *DHSS priorities document.* The DHSS Document appears to have been written by two rather different authors or groups of authors. First, there is the programme budget which must have been put together by the Department's economists and on which the Document relies for its statement of the present allocation of resources to the various programmes. Their views about the programme budget are, however, not mentioned until pages

78–84 (the last six pages of the document) and are added as a kind of appendix. In this, they state that 'the programme budget is neither a forecast nor a plan, it is a way of exploring possible future strategies for development, in this instance for the period 1979/80'. It seems therefore, that the economists were under the impression that the figures were to be used on a consultation basis and that they (the figures) were likely to be changed on the basis of this consultation. Certainly the forecasts and setting of priorities are not seen as being in any way fixed. This appendix also admits to major problems of excluding certain activities that fell without the defined area of public expenditure at a national aggregate level, and also admits that there are certain groups of services cutting across administrative boundaries, particularly the elderly and the physically handicapped. They write 'All home nursing and geriatric medicine are included in the "elderly" programme, and health visiting (but not paediatrics which cannot be costed separately) under "children"'. Towards the end of the appendix, they write 'It cannot be stressed too strongly that the figures are not accurate (to the extent of £1 million). The projections are presented as a quantitative illustration of the priorities put forward in this document they are not a detailed plan. The priorities are themselves still subject to consultation, but even if they were not, it would be quite impossible to place this degree of accuracy this far ahead at a national aggregate level'. The authors also admit to making some fairly sensitive assumptions concerning wage drift and current unit costs, implying therefore that charges will rise as fast as costs in the areas of local authority residential and day care. 'Nevertheless', they write, 'it is felt that the figures are sufficiently accurate for a broad *exploration* of priorities.' (My emphasis.)

The second group of authors of the DHSS priorities document would seem to be those responsible for allocation of funds who seem to have been engaged on a cunning piece of expediency whichever way we look at it. On the very first page of the introduction and summary we get a slightly different view of the purpose of the consultative document: 'It is intended that the strategy outlined in this document should provide health and local authorities with a basis for their own planning work and review of priorities starting in 1976', and although the introduction to the document does mention the need to change priorities as needs and strategies develop, the overall tone of the first 76 pages or so is that consultation is more about discussing the means by which authorities will meet the priorities in the document rather than consultation about the priorities and the figures provided in the document itself. If we adopt a particularly cynical view of the document and its proposals to allocate what resources there are to the elderly and general practice and away from acute medicine, we may make the following observation. If acute hospital medicine is effective, and if resources to this area are reduced, then we may expect that two things may occur. First, that those patients who, with continued financial support to the acute services might have been made more healthy and returned to work, may now stay on sickness benefit, particularly during a time of high unemployment. Secondly, that because people will be less fit and less healthy, they will be less likely to live as long, and therefore the problem of the elderly will be to some extent reduced. Given the observations by Williams and Rathwell that 'home helps, meals and day-centre provision will require 40–65 years before the targets (in the DHSS document) are achieved at the given growth rates', (Williams, C.J.H. and Rathwell, T.A., 1976), such a cynical view may not be so misplaced.

Reference to the article by Williams and Rathwell brings us to the point of the reliability of the method and the statistics in the Priorities Document. Two other articles have drawn attention to its unreliability. The first by Professor Knox of Birmingham, draws attention to the misplaced antithesis of primary care versus specialist care, and he writes 'No evidence on this particular issue is supplied, there is no reference to the relative effectiveness of general and specialist services, and the question of the balance between the two is evidently not up for discussion. It is pre-empted and rational discussion is prejudiced rather than assisted' (Knox, E.G., 1976).

More importantly, Knox draws attention to the fact that the effects of reallocation are largely discussed in terms of those services to which resources will be allocated rather than taken away. There is very little discussion in the document, he says, of the costs of reallocation away from acute hospital care.

The second article to question the DHSS document was produced by the Radical Statistics Health Group (RSHG, 1976), and reviewed in the *Lancet*. The Radical Statistics Health Group sees the consultative document 'as a smoke-screen to obscure the cuts in public expenditure and it makes a convincing case' (Lancet, 1976). As the review goes on to point out, the group does question some of the statistics on which the priorities document is based, in particular the growth rates for health centres, the mentally ill and pharmaceutical services, but their major concern is to question the effectiveness of certain procedures and also to question the assumptions contained in the document 'Prevention and Health—Everybody's Business' (DHSS, 1976c), which they see as putting the onus for prevention on to the individual and largely as ignoring the fact that much greater sums of money are spent on encouraging habits leading to disease (particularly smoking) rather than on health education, and that it ignores areas where legislation would certainly produce improvements. The Group concludes that the management approach embodied in the consultative document 'totally ignores both major questions as to the shape of the service and the wider social changes which will be needed if we are to make any real improvements in the health of the population' (RSHG, 1976).

My personal views about the publication of the DHSS document and the continuing discussion are at variance with both those of Knox and the Radical Statistics Health Group. It seems to me that this has been the first time that a document has been put together which has tried to allocate the various activities to their various services, and to estimate the monetary values involved. As such, this seems to be a step in the right direction and if the actual numbers are not correct, then it is to be regretted that the document has been used less as a consultative argument and more as a manipulative one.

We should, however, be grateful for the information that is contained in the document and for the argument it has provoked. The DHSS document itself argues that 'it is essential that (choice) should be made in full knowledge of the facts facing the services as a whole: the likely changes in demand by different client groups, the areas where past neglect has led to serious deficiencies, etc.' (DHSS, 1976a). The Radical Statistics Group argues that

> The DHSS should take into account the fact which the present document fails adequately to deal with that the health and personal social services are only some of the factors which influence health and well-being. All the available evidence about the effectiveness of the services influencing health should be evaluated, and further evidence collected if necessary. All this information should be made public and a form of consultation which is real and democratic should take place. Only then will we all be in a position to decide how to allocate our financial resources for the benefit of all' (RSHG 1976).

I would agree with the Radical Statistics Health Group that we do not have all the information, but it does seem to me that the consultative document was at least a start and has probably provoked interest into those factors which may be influential and which previously have not been measured or evaluated. However, their conclusion that 'all this information should be made public and a form of consultation which is real and democratic should take place', is at odds with Knox's argument that 'the only consistent arrangement of the preferences of a group of people is one which is imposed. This theorem deserves to be more widely studied, despite the unwelcome character of its implications' (Knox, E. G., 1976).

A (ii). *How to set priorities in medicine* (Comaish, J.S. 1976). Dr Comaish argues that there is little evidence or reasoning put forward to support the DHSS document's arguments for allocation, and he proposes an allocation formula based on prevalence, severity and curability. As a concise and rational system for the allocation of money, manpower and materials in the health service, Dr Comaish's formula is extremely attractive. By and large he is suggesting an advanced form of programme budgeting which incorporates health status indices as well—i.e. measures of outcome and effectiveness. The programmes he chooses are subdivided into disease groupings and this raises the first of the problems which I want to consider.

Those working on programme budgeting have begun their work with the desire to use disease groupings, but each one has found it to be unworkable in practice. We have already seen that in the very broad groups adopted by the DHSS document there were problems of definition and allocation to a particular group— particularly in the area of geriatric medicine (and why does such an important division not figure in Comaish's example?)—and these problems of definition are compounded every time a category is sub-divided. Comaish also argues, towards the end of his paper, that 'it would not be too lengthy a task to construct a scheme based on similar considerations of prevalence, severity, and curability applicable to primary health care and the personal social services'. However much I would like to agree with Comaish on this point, after some years working with general practitioners and hospital doctors, I do not believe that we are much nearer to constructing such a scheme or formula. My feelings are much closer to those of J. D. Pole when he writes:

A major complication is the fact that some programmes ought really to cover the personal social services as well as the health service. Social workers tend to take a broader view than doctors; they deal in syndromes. Even when there is a well defined task for the personal social services the objectives of care as seen by the social worker or other social services professional may be quite different from those perceived by a doctor considering the same case. On the whole the objectives of medical care fall into reasonably well-defined categories—preventing mortality, morbidity, disability, pain—but those of the personal social services are vaguer or perhaps more subtle (Pole, J.D., 1974).

Moving to the three factors on which Comaish bases his formula, he dismisses Abel-Smith's pessimism that 'epidemiological knowledge is at present far too limited for its use in health planning' (Abel-Smith, B., 1976) by arguing that 'Pessimism is always useless and nearly always proves wrong'. Whilst again wishing to agree with Comaish it does seem to me that at present we are largely unaware of the prevalence of particular diseases at any one time and it is also disturbing that Comaish does not consider the question of the *incidence* of a particular disease at any one time. We must also know, if we are to plan sensibly, whether prevalence and incidence are increasing or decreasing *over* time.

I should admit to being very excited by seeing a doctor considering ideas of measuring severity and curability, and take his point that 'doctors daily assess the degree of disability in claimants for injury or disability benefit, and the panels and appeals tribunals appointed by the DHSS come to decisions which though arbitrary are based on careful scrutiny of the total effect of many different diseases on peoples' lives'. In fact research into applying exactly this type of analysis to hospital output has been going on for some time (Rosser, R.M. & Watts, V.C., 1972; 1975). These researchers found their method of classifying disability and distress by different doctors and across the specialties of general surgery, general medicine, ophthalmology, physical medicine, ENT, gynaecology, urology and psychiatry, to be largely repeatable and consistent. They also found that they were able to cover most of the categories of disability and distress with suitable legal cases and thereby be able to scale disability and distress. As the authors admit, however, the figures they produce for their own hospital (a 300-bedded general hospital which became part of Guy's in 1967) are not meaningful in isolation. 'It is the possibility of seeing how they change over time at St Olave's and of comparing St Olave's with other hospitals which makes them potentially valuable.' Rosser and Watts have not, as far as I know, taken their work into the field of programme budgeting and the Comaish type formula, but its techniques are obviously valuable and encouraging. Comaish's comment that 'the sympathetic and careful balancing of all factors will be a hard task for a group of even very wise men, but a soluble one given the resources of modern sociology and epidemiology' may be encouraging for those of us who work in departments of medical sociology and epidemiology, but in spite of my harsh comments about health economics, it would seem obvious that they should also be added to this group: economists have been at the forefront of research in this area.

Comaish goes on to consider curability, and although he does at least recognise that time will affect this factor of curability (and adds 'amendment of the prevalence and severity factors would also be required'), he does not stop to dwell on the obvious lack of information we have on clinical outcome and effectiveness in both hospital and primary health care. From the economist's point of view, Comaish fails to consider the relationship between inputs and outputs—in other words that curability may be increased by increasing the amount of one particular resource devoted to one unit of through-put, or that substitution of inputs may improve curability (see Knox's argument).

In a letter to the *Lancet* subsequent to this article, Comaish replied to a critic that severity includes costs to everyone—costs to the patient, to the patient's family and cost to the hospital (Comaish, J.S., 1976b). I personally feel that this is a confusing argument and that it would be more helpful if severity referred to patient costs and that a new variable 'health service cost', be added to his formula.

Comaish's article is both encouraging and provocative, particularly as it comes from the medical profession itself, but we all need to be on our guard lest we have too great expectations of what can be evaluated and apportioned over a feasible time period. Whatever we may like to believe, the economist's, sociologist's, and epidemiologist's data and techniques are at present inadequate as the basis for applying Dr Comaish's formula. We should beware lest our wishful thinking becomes a measurability myth.

But Dr Comaish's paper must also be considered for its value standpoint. Having commented on the 'imperious decrees' which have no visible means of support in the DHSS document, Dr Comaish certainly provides detailed reasoning for his formula, but we should be aware of the value-judgments contained in his paper. In the first place he assumes a service that is generally similar to that being provided today, and whilst his model would allow us to take account of regional inequalities in the provision of health care services, it does not at all cope with class inequalities except where they are regionally important and at no time does he suggest a means for allocating resources to those of the lower social classes whom we know to have poorer health (Blaxter, M., 1976; Brotherston, J., 1976; Cartwright, A. & O'Brien, M., 1976). In fact, Comaish's paper suffers from the same value-judgments that the Radical Statistics Health Group identifies in the DHSS priorities document.

B. *Financing and paying for health services.* The Royal College of Physicians of Edinburgh Symposium on Economic Consider-ations in the Health Service (RCPE, 1977) reflected the concern that doctors have about the amount of money flowing to the health care sector, and there were a few references to alternative methods of financing health services. The economist chosen to speak to the conference made the valid observation that at the early stages of illness many people choose to self-medicate by going to the chemist, which is a form of private health service. He went on to suggest that services 'for the avoidance of death' should be publicly funded and 'services for the avoidance of un-pleasantness' should be met out of private funds. Such a sugges-tion seems to me to be amazingly naive both in terms of being able to categorise those services which might be labelled 'death avoidance' and those that might be labelled 'unpleasantness avoidance'. Obviously the extremes are easily identifiable, but there is a large grey area in the middle where I am sure very few doctors would like to distinguish between the two. Such a scheme would also be likely to run into many of the troubles that beset the United States health service—problems of queue jumping, of gross over-provision of certain services and under-provision of others and of discrimination against those least able to pay. From this point of view it was encouraging to hear that a two-tiered health service was politically unrealistic, largely because, private medicine would not campaign for those most in need, which were identified as the elderly and the handicapped.

The question of misuse of the service occurred at the conference a number of times and it was suggested that the costs of using health services should be made known to users. This was one argument for a private health service. The general principle of knowing the cost of the service being bought is, I believe, valid and more information should be provided to the public about the cost of the health service and the costs of using different parts of that service. At the same time, however, it is important that the public is aware of the mechanism for complaint when it is felt that the services provided are not of a sufficiently high standard.

My final point is one I consider to be crucial but unresolved. Basically it centres on thoughts about individual responsibility for health.

In the first of the addresses to the conference held by the Royal College of Physicians, of Edinburgh, attention was drawn not only to the problems that will be created by the large number of elderly in Scotland in a few years time but also to three major causes of mortality—accidents, cancer of the lung and ischaemic heart disease. The implication of what was said was that all of these were largely treatable only from the health prevention angle and by health education, and this is the point that ties in with the brief observation made about the DHSS priorities document. It would seem that as medical science has advanced and as actuarial skills have developed, so we are moving into a situation where individuals are being held responsible for their own health and that this is a significant move from the principles embodied in the founding of the NHS when it was argued that ill-health could strike any of us at any time without prior warning. There was evidence of this shift of values and assessment of individual responsibility in the Government's proposals to move the payment of medical care services resulting from car accidents outwith the National Health Service. I have however two points to be discussed.

First, while I wholeheartedly welcome any moves which encourage the individual patient to take responsibility for his own health, we should be aware that the present social structure seldom encourages individual responsibility towards society in general. (Wedderburn, D. & Craig, C., 1974; *Observer*, 1977). The issue may not be so much one of class (as defined in the Registrar-General's classification of occupations), but rather as one of power, be it employer or trade-union, both of which may work in the interests of power holders rather than those 'on the shop floor'. When this is added to our knowledge of different uses of language by different social classes (Bernstein, B., 1970) and the continuing importance of the historical location of social classes (Goldthorpe, J.H. *et al.*, 1968), then we should not be surprised that preventive medicine and health education have little appeal to a large section of the British population, in particular those often in most need as defined medically. In other words, I am suggesting that it is unrealistic of health service planners to expect people to make responsible decisions about their health when the whole of their life styles and the situations in which they find themselves in society do not encourage such behaviour. Therefore, solutions to these three main causes of mortality—accidents, cancer of the lung and ischaemic heart disease—whilst being an individual's responsibility, have a major social component. If we wish to see mortality reduced then there has to be a major change in the social structure.

My second point relates again to the social structure, but in this case to the point that is well made in the Guy's document; namely, that much of industry actually creates ill health (Draper, P. *et al.*, 1976). We should not, I feel, focus all our attention on those illnesses which are the responsibility of the individual and we should recognise that public and industrial health can all be improved, at some cost to society. Asbestosis is, of course, a classic example.

To conclude, there are still issues of justice, freedom and economic efficiency which require considerably more discussion than has yet taken place before we put too much trust in the panacea opened up by planners' techniques:

A few years ago a physician speculated on what, based on current knowledge, would be the composite picture of an individual with a low risk of developing atherosclerosis or coronary-artery disease. He would be: . . . an effeminate municipal worker or embalmer completely lacking in physical or mental alertness and without drive, ambition, or competitive spirit; who has never attempted to meet a deadline of any kind; a man with poor appetite, subsisting on fruit and vegetables laced with corn and whale oil, detesting tobacco, spurning ownership of radio, television, or motorcar, with full head of hair but scrawny and unathletic appearance, yet constantly straining his puny muscles by exercise. Low in income, blood pressure, blood sugar, uric acid and cholesterol, he has been taking nicotinic acid, pyridoxine and long-term anti-coagulant therapy ever since his prophylactic castration (Zola, I.K., 1971).

REFERENCES

Abel-Smith, B. (1976) *Value for Money in Health Services.*

Bernstein, B. (1970) 'Education cannot Compensate for Society', *The Sociology of Modern Britain* (1975), ed. Butterworth and Weir.

Blaxter, M. (1976) 'Social Class and Health Inequalities' in *Equalities and Inequalities in Health*, ed. Carter, C.O. and Peel, J.

British Medical Journal (1975) Leader, i, p. 593.

Brooks, R. (1971) 'A cost-benefit analysis of the treatment of rheumatic diseases', *Applied Economics*, vol. 3, pp. 35-53.

Brotherston. J. (1976) 'The Galton Lecture, 1975: Inequality, Is it inevitable' in *Equalities and Inequalities in Health*, ed. Carter, C.O. and Peel, J.

Buxton, M.J. and West, R.R. (1975) 'Cost benefit analysis of Long-Term Haemodialysis for Chronic Renal Failure', *BMJ*, 2, pp. 376-9.

Carter, F. *et al.* (1976) 'Cost of Management of Patients with Haemophilia, *BMJ*, 2, pp. 465-7.

Cartwright, A. and O'Brien, M. (1976) 'Social Class variation in Health Care . . .' in *The Sociology of the NHS*, ed. Stacey, M., Sociological Review Monograph, No. 22.

Cohen, R.H.L. (1971) 'The Department's role in research and development' in *Portfolio for Health*, ed. McLachlan, G.

Comaish, J. S. (1976a) 'How to set priorities in medicine', *Lancet*, ii, p. 512.
Comaish, J. S.(1976b) Letter to *Lancet*, ii, p. 797.
Culyer, A. J. *et al.* (1971) 'Social Indicators: Health', reproduced from
  Social Trends, No. 2, pp. 31-42.
Culyer, A. J. (1976) *Need and the National Health Service.*
Davies, G. M. (1973) 'Fluoride in the prevention of dental caries', *British
  Dental Journal*, Aug. 21, pp. 173-4.
DHSS (1976a) *Priorities for Health and Personal Social Services in England.*
  HMSO.
DHSS (1976b) *Sharing Resources for Health in England.* Report of the
  Resource Allocation Working Party. HMSO.
DHSS (1976c) *Prevention and Health—Everybody's Business.* HMSO.
Draper, P. *et al.* (1976) *Health, Money and the National Health Service.* Unit
  for the Study of Health Policy. Guy's Hospital Medical School.
Fein, R. (1971) 'On Measuring Economic Benefits of Health Programmes'
  in *Medical History and Medical Care*, ed. McLachlan, G. and
  McKeown, T.
Feldstein, M. S. (1967) *Economic Analysis for Health Service Efficiency.*
Glass, N. J. (1973) 'Cost-Benefit Analysis and Health Services', *Health
  Trends*, 5, 3, pp. 51-6.
Glass, N. J. and Russell, I. T. (1974) 'Cost-benefit Analysis in the Health
  Service: A Case Study of Elective Herniorrhaphy', *British Journal of
  Preventive and Social Medicine*, vol. 28, p. 68.
Goldthorpe, J. H. *et al.* (1968) *The Affluent Worker.*
Grogono, A. W. and Woodgate, D. J. (1971) 'Index for measuring Health',
  Lancet, ii, pp. 1024-6.
Hawgood, J. and Morley, R. (1969) *Project for Evaluating the Benefits from
  University Libraries.* University of Durham.
Illich, I. (1976) *Limits to Medicine.*
Jennett, B. (1976) *Lancet*, ii, p. 1235.
Jones-Lee, M. W. (1973) 'Revealed Preferences and the Value of a Life' in
  Health Economics, ed. Cooper, M. H. and Culyer, A. J.
Jonsson, B. (1976) 'The Evaluation of Alternative Treatments for Gall-
  Stones'. Paper presented to Health Economists Study Group, July 1976
  (unpublished).
Klarman, H. E. (1965) 'Syphilis control programs' in *Measuring Benefits of
  Government Investments*, ed. Dorfman, R.
Klarman, H. E. *et al.* (1968) 'Cost effectiveness analysis applied to the
  treatment of chronic renal disease', *Medical Care*, vol. 6, pp. 48-54.
Knox, E. G. (1976) 'Priorities for Health—A Manipulative Document?',
  Lancet, Oct. 9th, p. 790.
Lancet (1976) ii, p. 1035.
Lavers, R. J. (1972) 'The Implicit Valuation of Forms of Hospital Treatment'
  in *The Economics of Medical Care*, ed. Hauser, M. M.
McKeown, T. (1976) *The Role of Medicine.*
Mills, C. W. (1959) *The Sociological Imagination.*
Mills, M. (1976) 'The application of cost-benefit analysis to health services—
  Some Problems raised by an Evaluation of Flexible Fibreoptic
  Endoscopes: Paper presented to the Health Economists Study Group in
  July 1976 (unpublished).
Mishan, E. J. (1977) *The Economic Growth Debate.*
Mooney, G. (1976) Transcript of speech to conference on Health Services
  Economics at Scottish Health Service Centre, Edinburgh, on Thursday,
  26th February 1976.

127

Appendix 1

Morley, R. (1972) 'Comment on "The Implicit Valuation of Forms of Hospital Treatment"' in *The Economics of Medical Care*, ed. Hauser, M.M.

Navarro, V. (1976) *Medicine under Capitalism*.

Observer (1977) 'Journey Into the Working Class', 16th January.

Piachaud, D. and Weddell, J.M. (1972) 'The Economics of treating Varicose Veins', *International Journal of Epidemiology*, vol. 1, No. 3, pp. 287-93.

Pole, J.D. (1972) 'The Economics of Mass Radiography' in *The Economics of Medical Care*, ed. Hauser, M.M.

Pole, J.D. (1974) 'Programmes, Priorities and Budgets' in *British Journal of Preventive and Social Medicine*, 28, pp. 191-5.

Porter, A.M.D. (1971) *Planning Maternity Care*. Unpublished M.Phil. thesis, University of Durham.

Radical Statistics Health Group (1976) *Whose Priorities?* (c/o BSSRS, 9 Poland St., London W1).

Rex, J. (1974) *Sociology and the Demystification of the Modern World*.

Reynell, R.C. and Reynell, M.C. (1972) 'The Cost-Benefit Analysis of a Coronary Care Unit' *British Heart Journal*, vol. 34, pp. 897-900.

Rich, G. *et al.* (1976) 'The Cost-effectiveness of two methods of screening for asymptomatic bacteriuria', *British Journal of Preventive and Social Medicine*, 30, pp. 54-9.

Rosser, R.M. and Watts, V.C. (1972) The Measurement of Hospital Output' *International Journal of Epidemiology*, vol. 1, No. 4, pp. 361-8.

Rosser, R.M. and Watts, V.C. (1975) 'Disability—A Clinical Classification', *New Law Journal*, April 3rd, p. 323.

Royal College of Physicians of Edinburgh Conference held on February 3rd, 1977.

Salter, H.C. (1972) 'Public Expenditure and the Health and Welfare Services' in *The Economics of Medical Care*, ed. Hauser, M.M.

SHHD (1976) *The Way Ahead*. HMSO.

SSRC Health Economists Group (Various years) Institute of Economic and Social Research, University of York.

Teeling-Smith, G.E. (1972) 'A Cost-Benefit Approach to Medical Care' in *The Economics of Medical Care*, ed. Hauser, M.M.

Wager, R. (1972) *Care of the Elderly*—An exercise in cost-benefit analysis commissioned by Essex County Council. IMTA, London.

Wedderburn, D. and Craig, C. (1974) 'Relative Deprivation in Work', *Poverty, Inequality and Class Structure*, ed. Wedderburn.

Weissbrod, B.A. (1975) 'Research in Health Economics: A Survey', *International Journal of Health Services*, vol. 5, No. 6, pp. 643-61.

Williams, A.H. (1972) 'Foreword' to *The Economics of Medical Care*, ed. Hauser, M.M.

Williams, A.H. (1974a) 'Measuring the Effectiveness of Health Care Systems' in *The Economics of Health and Medical Care*, ed. Perlman, M.

Williams, A.H. (1974b) 'The Cost-Benefit Approach', *British Medical Bulletin*, vol. 30, No. 3, pp. 252-6.

Williams, A.H. (1975) 'What can economists do to help Health Service planning?'. Paper presented to the Association of University Teachers of Economics (unpublished).

Williams, C.J.H. and Rathwell, T.A. (1976) 'Could the consultative document have its priorities wrong?' *BMJ*, October 16th, p. 956.

Zola, I.K. (1971) 'Medicine as an Institution of Social Control' reprinted in *A Sociology of Medical Practice*, ed. Cox and Mead.

Since this paper was completed, a number of relevant articles and books have been published or brought to my notice:

Mooney, G. H. (1977) *The Valuation of Human Life.*

Mooney, G. H. (1977) 'Programme Budgeting in an Area Health Board', *The Hospital and Health Services Review*, November.

Caird, W. I. and Mooney, G. H. (1977) 'What is the monetary value of a human life', *BMJ*, 2, pp. 1627-9.

Ferster, G. and Butts, M. (1977) 'A Method for estimating revenue expenditure by specialty in an RHA', *The Hospital and Health Services Review*, March.

Ferster, G. and Butts, M. (1977) 'An Analysis of Specialty Costs in an NHS Region', *The Hospital and Health Services Review*, November.

Black, D. A. K. (1977) 'Cui Bono?', *BMJ*, 2, pp. 1109-14.

Rickard, J. H. (1976) *Cost-effectiveness analysis of the Oxford Community Hospital Programme.* Health Services Evaluation Group. Department of the Regius Professor of Medicine. University of Oxford.

One book which should have been included in the review but which was cut out during revision of the paper is that by Cooper, M. H. (1975) *Rationing Health Care.*

2

PRACTICE: DECISIONS AND RESOURCES IN THE NATIONAL HEALTH SERVICE (SCOTLAND)

The research was prompted by two concerns:

(a) little is known about the dynamics of the decision-making process in the NHS at the local level (by local I mean the field authorities below the central department: fifteen health boards (i.e. field authorities) are directly responsible to the Scottish Home & Health Department (SHHD);

(b) puzzlement at the persistence of resource imbalances between different sectors of health care provision, despite attempts by successive governments to redress these.

(a) *The dynamics of decision making.* This situation in part reflects the lack of decision-making studies in the field of Public Administration generally—there are few case studies of how administrators go about their work. A great deal of the existing literature tends to be legalistic and institutional in its orientation, and centres on structural questions—size of authorities, distribution of powers and so on—rather than on actual behaviour within these structures. There is not much literature on the dynamics of decision-making and the political realities involved in decision processes. Books on public administration, as Ridley (1972) has noted, 'embody little research into what actually goes on inside the administration. . . . The administration . . . is the box in which inputs are actually translated into outputs. . . . The way the box is organised, its pattern of work and communication system, for example, is bound to affect (the policy process)'. A real understanding of the administration of the NHS at local level can only come from studying 'the decision-making process in its managerial as well as its political aspects' (pp. 70–1). I hasten to add that these remarks apply only to the United Kingdom. The situation in America is quite different. Nevertheless, there are some exceptions in this country—for example, Kogan's (1975) study of educational policy-making; Chapman's (1968) slim volume on the decision to raise the Bank Rate in 1957; Heclo and

Wildavsky's (1974) apposite observations of the British civil service. However, all these studies are concerned with macro-policy-making at the national level. At a more micro level, the Institute for Operational Research has produced two interesting studies, Friend and Jessop (1969) and Friend *et al.* (1974).

Despite the exceptions I have just mentioned, in general, decision-making is unexplored terrain. In particular, there is a great deal of ignorance about decision-making processes at the local level in the NHS in Scotland. The Farquharson-Lang (1966) report on administrative practice in hospital boards did provide some useful, though limited, structural information on the composition and operations of Regional Hospital Boards (RHBS) and Boards of Management (BOMS), but since the reorganisation of the NHS in 1974 even these inadequate data are now out-of-date. In England work has been, and is being, done at Hull, Leeds and at Brunel (to name but three university centres) in some of these neglected areas. The work produced by the Institute for Health Studies at Hull University has been particularly interesting (see Brown *et al.*, 1975). However, in my opinion, Scotland merits separate attention if only because the structure of the Scottish Health Service is different in several important respects from the English structure. Moreover, very little research concerned with organisational questions or decision-making processes has been undertaken in the NHS in Scotland. I am aware of only two projects, IOR (1976) and Taylor (1977).

It is perhaps worth mentioning at this point that there have been some studies of NHS policy-making on a national level (see Klein, 1974a and b), but these have only served to emphasise the paucity of data about what goes on within health authorities on the periphery. It was Maurice Kogan (1976) who wrote recently that 'social scientists in this country are far too interested in large-scale decision-making at the centre to come to grips with the fine grain of social systems and what they have to do. Such questions as . . . the structure of the delivery system, the ways in which different values can be stated in the hum-drum institutions that make up the welfare state are the real base line for policy analysis . . .' (p. 491). My research is an example of this approach to decision-making analysis.

(b) *Resource imbalances*. I am thinking here primarily of those imbalances which occur *within* health authorities rather than those which exist *between* different parts of the UK. Why is it that acute services continue to receive the bulk of available resources, while the 'Cinderella' sectors (geriatrics, the mentally ill, the mentally handicapped) continue to lag behind? I am interested in the factors and/or constraints which operate in the decision process to account for this situation.

For example, do the imbalances which exist between services arise from the power relations within health boards (e.g. medical dominance of decision-making by prestigious specialists)? Do they emanate from a desire not to disturb vested interests? Or do they perhaps exist as a result of the uncertainty of the environment: decision-makers simply do not know what to do or how to do it? Heclo (1975) has written that 'social policy-making is about puzzlement as well as power; it entails both knowing and deciding' (p. 152). It may be that in an uncertain environment, administrators strive for stability and order rather than encourage change or innovation, and hence the tendency to maintain the *status quo*. Schon (1971) has termed this reaction 'dynamic conservatism' (i.e. people fight like mad to stay where they are). It is not simply a question of medical politics dictating what decisions emerge, although undeniably such activity is of relevance. The process is more subtle than crude power politics. The NHS decision-making environment is, or certainly can be, uncertain. Preventive care illustrates this. No one is quite sure what preventive care means or involves in the way of specific policies and services. Is a health education programme worth initiating? Or should mass screening programmes be started? How does one measure a return on investment? How does one know if preventive services are doing the job expected of them? The entire preventive field is riddled with such questions—answers may be forthcoming one day, but meantime administrators and others are involved in what might be termed 'cautious groping'.

An interesting point is raised when one discusses the imbalances in service provision that occur within health authorities. This is that decision-making in the NHS is far more decentralised than is sometimes argued. For example, Enoch Powell, when Minister of Health, maintained that the NHS was overcentralised, whereas Richard Crossman, when he was Secretary of State for Health and Social Services, believed quite vehemently that the centre lacked sufficient control over health authorities. And, in fact, the reorganisation of the NHS is in large part an attempt to improve the centre's ability to decide overall priorities and influence the decisions taken by the field authorities. I would argue that decision-making in the NHS is indeed decentralised and that health authorities possess a large measure of influence over the services they provide. It is at this level where that health policy is largely formulated and implemented. And it is for this reason that a study into the operations of these authorities is worth-while. Similar myths about centralisation and the erosion of local autonomy surround the relationship between central and local government. Whereas the report of the Layfield Committee on Local Government Finance supports this orthodox view, some observers, including Rhodes (Layfield, Appendix 6, 1976), believe that it is misleading. There is a distinction between the controls central government has over local government and their actual operation. 'Legal forms and reality differ markedly' (p. 184). What needs to be recognised is the political dimension: '. . . complex interactions take place within a system of *administrative politics* . . .' (p. 187). Just as local authorities should be seen as political systems, so should health authorities.

STUDY AIMS

The case study has two aims, both of which stem from the two concerns which prompted the research:

(a) The study is a description of decision-making in two health boards. It is concerned with discovering the processes by which certain policy decisions are made in the NHS at this local level by seeking answers to questions like: how are scarce resources allocated? Who is involved in these decisions? How are choices made between competing demands? Is there a hierarchy of power or influence? What information is used in the discussions surrounding the decision-making process? In short, the case study is an attempt to look into the 'black box' which comprises the decision process.

(b) The study is a profile of the reorganised NHS in Scotland. The research, it is hoped, will provide some insights into the operation of the new management structure within health boards.

CASE STUDY AND ITS FOCUS ON
DEVELOPMENT FUND ALLOCATIONS

There are two ways of designing a research project: (a) top-down approach; (b) bottom-up approach. In (a), the researcher selects hypotheses, tests these, and tries to falsify them. This is the scientific, positivist approach to research design. In (b), the researcher enters a field with no hypotheses or preconceptions and develops theory from direct observation. This is the inductive method and the 'grounded theory' approach is an example of this kind of research design. Each approach presents difficulties and I have attempted to combine elements from both in order to overcome some of the problems. I do not want to get involved in a theoretical discussion at present: suffice it to say that the questions which the case study attempts to answer have been guided by some explicit theoretical assumptions, derived mainly from rational and incremental theories, as well as by many vague ideas obtained from the literature on the NHS, and from my own early experiences in the field.

It is not possible for one researcher to observe the whole decision-making process in a health board, so I decided to select a well-defined area on which to concentrate my efforts. I focused on a particular set of resource-allocation decisions. Wildavsky (1964) claims that the task of allocating money can explain, or help to explain, how people at various levels in an organisation co-operate, bargain, and negotiate. This, in turn, can tell us much about the administrative structure of an organisation—its operation and the interaction among its component parts. A study of resource-allocation decisions can indicate what pressures make for *policy change* or for *policy maintenance* (see Dearlove, 1973) and from where these originate.

It was during exploratory discussions with health board officers that I decided to observe the allocation of development funds (DF), particularly in the area of staffing. This is an interesting area to study since DF represent the 'new' money each health board receives annually from the SHHD.

This 'new' money enables a health board to develop new services, improve existing ones, or to change direction as a result of the particular emphasis placed on certain services. The greater part of the total allocation to health boards is already earmarked for existing commitments. Although theoretically these funds could be put to different uses, in practice they are not. The budgets remain fixed—in the jargon there are no 'zero-base reviews'. This explains why DF are viewed with such significance (although now that DF are practically non-existent and will remain so for some time, managers are having to begin to examine the use made of existing resources in order to see if any 'slack' can be identified which can be taken up by reallocating resources from one sector to another). In a Service which has been accustomed to an annual growth rate of between $2\frac{1}{2}$ and 5 per cent, DF are very important. In a climate where expansion has been the norm these funds are eagerly relied upon. Naturally, there are many competing claims on them and they far outweigh the funds available for disbursement.

I have been concerned primarily with those DF which have gone on increases in staff establishments (i.e. recurring revenue allocations). I do not need to point out that the NHS is a labour-intensive organisation in which 75 per cent of expenditure goes on wages and salaries (and over half of this total goes on doctors' and nurses' salaries). It is obvious that expenditure on staff represents a vitally important area of decision-making—decisions taken in this area dictate the direction in which the Service as a whole moves. For example, if more funds are allocated to recruiting health visitors and nursing auxiliaries for domiciliary care than are allocated to recruiting more hospital nurses, then it is possible to say that the Service is moving in the direction of providing better community care facilities and that this is where a board's priority lies. Decisions on staffing are a commitment on future resources. If a consultant is appointed, for example, he will create more work, he will require additional supporting staff, he will add to the burdens on nursing, on laboratory facilities and so on.

The two health boards I chose for the case study were selected on a number of criteria, none of which is particularly scientific. The difficulty is that each of the fifteen health boards has its own peculiar characteristics and it is not possible to pinpoint a typical health board. They range in population size from over 1 million (Greater Glasgow) to 17,000 (Orkney). A cluster of boards falls within the population range of between 300,000 and 450,000. The membership of boards also varies, ranging from twenty-two members in the larger boards to fourteen members in the smaller ones.

I settled on two medium-sized boards which have comparable demographic characteristics, a mix of urban-industrial and rural health problems, and similar organisational structures (both are divided into two Districts). I selected these health boards for their similarities rather than for points of contrast so as to ascertain whether what I was observing in one board was unique to that board or whether it resembled what was happening in the other board.

PRELIMINARY FINDINGS

Two sets of findings are emerging from the case study (it must be remembered that analysis of the data is at present incomplete) and these are closely linked to the study aims I outlined earlier.

(a) *Allocation Process and DF*

As a general observation, it would not be unfair to describe the decision-making process I looked at as consisting largely of administering and maintaining an ongoing system rather than of making fundamental changes in it. Much of the discussion about

135

change and the need to set new priorities which may lead to large-scale changes, or necessitate such changes (like a commitment to preventive care), tends to remain at the level of symbolic posturing ('coffee table chat') rather than become realised in actual allocation decisions. Change can, and sometimes does, occur marginally through incremental improvements and expansions, but developments usually mean 'more of the same' rather than significant new departures. In general, decision-making is biased towards *attending* to the arrangements of the health care system rather than towards *making* the arrangements (see Parry and Morriss, 1974). This mode of operation largely explains why the hospital service continues to absorb the bulk of available resources. The basic expenditure patterns have their origin in the days before the NHS was created and they have not been questioned over the years (until now, that is—see reports of DHSS's Resource Allocation Working Party, 1976 and SHHD's Working Party on Revenue Resource Allocation, 1977). The bulk of expenditure is simply re-enacted each year without being challenged. Now I am sure all this is familiar stuff to most of those involved. What one wants to know is *why* the system operates in this way. How do decision-makers *themselves* explain and account for their actions? I conceive of my research as being an attempt to reconstruct the DF allocation process as defined by decision-makers.

First, one must consider the environment within which NHS administrators and other decision-making participants operate, and examine the constraints imposed on them by this environment. Officers at Area and District levels of the health board structure are subjected to a number of constraints arising from without, as well as from within, the board itself. I'd like to consider some of these:

(i) *Existing Services*. A health board is stuck with the services it inherits from the past. Once services are established a board is committed to maintaining them, particularly when services very quickly gather momentum and are seen to be indispensable. This commitment to existing services and institutions can lead to anomalies. For example, in one of the boards I studied there are two large hospitals for the mentally ill which are too big for the needs of the area but which provide facilities for other parts of Scotland. The trouble is that hospitals of this type are usually severely understaffed and require constant attention. A Chief Area Nursing Officer (CANO) explained to me that in smallish boards DF are very important because financially these boards have little room to manoeuvre. 'Any improvement of psychiatric or mental deficiency services in my area depends totally on our development monies. They are vital because there is so little slack in existing services'.

(ii) *Time*. This is an obvious constraint which affects decision-makers in any organisation. Nevertheless, it is still a crucial constraint since quite a rigid timetable is adhered to in allocating DF. The quicker decisions are taken, the sooner funds can be spent and staff recruited, and the less chance there is of funds remaining unspent at the close of the financial year (or, alternatively, being spent on unnecessary items of furniture). Because of this tight timetable, administrators lack time to prepare detailed cases supporting every submission. Since District Officers usually possess more detailed information than their Area counterparts, most of the detailed allocation decisions occur at District level. This is a source of friction between the two tiers because the Area is in charge of broad planning and policy-making and yet it is not well-placed to argue the merits or otherwise of particular developments; nor has it the time to brief itself adequately on such matters.

(iii) *Lack of Information*. Information is sometimes available but may not be used because of the amount of time involved in assembling it. This results in greater weight being attached to the persuasiveness of a particular officer in putting a case for a development (at one District Executive Group (DEG) meeting, a heavier weighting was given to the District Nursing Officer's (DNO) case because her 'cri de coeur' seemed to be the loudest at that time and there was just no time to establish the known facts and figures). In deciding allocations the main types of information used are: staff/patient ratios, staffing numbers (reference is frequently made to Scottish Hospital Costs for comparative purposes with other similar hospitals), work-loads, waiting-lists and bed occupancy rates. These types of information do not necessarily provide reliable indicators of need and may reflect other factors like inefficient staff output. As Klein (1975) has argued, improving the NHS by adding to its manpower is only one possible policy option. Another option is to improve the use made of the NHS's manpower.

(iv) *Consultation*. There is a necessity to consult widely before final decisions on DF can be reached. Reorganisation has resulted in a plethora of professional advisory committees at all levels of the organisation (national, area and, in some boards, district). Seeking their approval for proposed developments is time-consuming. In a subtle way, these committees, by their very existence, make officers more cautious in the recommendations they put before the committees for comment. Officers, in an endeavour to avoid lengthy delays which could jeopardise the implementation of developments, are anxious not to cause offence to any group, least of all the medical profession.

(v) *Consensus Decision-Making*. The executive groups at Area and District levels operate as consensus-forming teams. There is no chief executive figure, although the Secretary at Area and the District Administrator (DA) at District do perform co-ordinating roles. Reaching unanimous agreement can on occasion take time. It can also prove awkward. A DA told me that at DF allocation meetings he felt in a confused position. He was confronted by three professional officers (District Medical Officer (DMO), DNO, and District Dental Officer), all claiming that their developments were top priority. The DA wondered who the arbiter was in this negotiating situation. It can't be him because the DA has to reach consensus with two of these professional officers (the DMO and DNO) who are, along with the DA and District Finance Officer (DFO), equal members of the DEG. Pre-reorganisation, the BOM could act as an arbiter, with the Secretary putting the choice to the board. Now, unless the DEG can agree among themselves, proposals go to the Area Executive Group (AEG). If they are unable to agree about something, then the matter goes to the full board (i.e. the final arbiter).

(vi) *Priority-Setting*. Officers experience great difficulty in placing requests in some order of priority. Requests for DF are banded into categories 'A', 'B', or 'C'. Problems arise in trying to decide between all the 'A's since most developments come into this category. For example, should a dental officer come before a nurse? Decisions about priorities between different disease or dependency groups pose complex problems since they require cross comparisons to be made between different groups of the population who are suffering from different conditions, and they raise fundamental value questions; for example, how do decision-makers compare providing care for an elderly person, with undertaking cardiac surgery for a middle-aged man suffering from heart disease? Decision-makers face these dilemmas when allocating DF and it is easy to reduce priority-setting to a matter of life and death criteria ('waving the shrouds').

In addition to these internal constraints, there are two important sets of external constraints:

(i) Although integration has occurred between primary care, hospital care, and community care, personal social services remain under local authority control. I have not observed liaison arrangements between health boards and local authorities but few officers seem to be enthusiastic about them or feel that they are of value in their present form. But there is no doubt that the policies local authorities pursue in relation to social work services can have a significant impact on the policies of health boards. For example, if a health board wishes to ease pressures on the hospital service, one way to achieve this is to expand community services. Home helps are an important element in any such policy but come under local authority control. The cuts in local government expenditure have had an effect on the provision of home helps which makes it much more difficult for health boards to speed up discharges from hospitals. Unlike England, no joint planning or joint financing arrangements exist in Scotland at present.

(ii) The SHHD imposes constraints on decision-makers in health boards, particularly in periods of resource shortages like the present. National policy decisions over Family Planning and junior doctors' salaries must be implemented by health boards without additional resources being made available to them for these purposes. At present, boards are also being asked by the SHHD to give priority to schemes with no running-cost implications. This means giving priority to developments which do not really warrant such favourable treatment. It also means reinforcing the institutional bias in health care provision, since, most of all, community services need to have their staff establishments improved.

Apart from, but largely because of, these constraints, the decision process surrounding DF allocations is fluid, random and messy. There exist no objective criteria for allocating the funds. Judgment, hunch, political fashion, public pressure (via media, especially local press and radio), pressure group influence, and the influence of official bodies like the Scottish Hospital Advisory Service (whose visits to long-stay institutions in the boards I studied did lead, in a number of minor cases, to changes being made in DF allocations so as to remedy deficiencies highlighted by the team from the Advisory Service) are the criteria commonly used. I think the fashionability of community care over the past few years illustrates some of these influences at work in the allocation process.

I said earlier that change was very difficult to bring about in health boards and that decisions reflected a commitment to an ongoing system of service provision. However, change is not impossible and the emphasis upon community health services in recent years is a good example of how change can occur, albeit gradually at the margin. During my period of observation a lot of stress was placed upon community health services and the need to expand them. A number of factors appeared to account for this which, in many ways, were unique to community care services:

(i) Many administrators in the NHS were acutely aware of a feeling among those running community services that reorganisation was nothing more than a takeover of the entire health service by the hospital service—health boards were looked upon as old RHBs in disguise. An obvious way of overcoming these fears and suspicions was to channel resources into community health services in order to show the good faith of the administrators and to prove to those working in community services that they had their interests very much at heart.

(ii) Many of the community services inherited by health boards from local health authorities in 1974 required a great deal of attention. Many had been seriously neglected and were substandard. Boards simply could not ignore these deficiencies which put community services in the category of 'poor relation' to the well-endowed hospital service.

(iii) The climate in the mid-1970s was just right. By 1974, community care had become politically fashionable and trendy. As the economic situation continued to deteriorate, while the cost of running the NHS continued to rise, the popularity of community care increased. Economic reasons prevailed although laced with humanitarian ideals. It was claimed to be cheaper to treat people at home, instead of putting them into costly hospital surroundings (this remains to be proven). In any case, institutionalising patients was demoralising and dehumanising. Reorganisation is in part an attempt to build up community services in order to relieve pressures on hospitals, particularly acute beds which are clogged up with long-stay patients who really ought not to be in hospital. With national politicians favouring community care, officers in the health boards responded accordingly. They had a clear objective to move towards and with which they were in complete agreement. Nevertheless, the possibility exists that this recent shift to community care may be short-lived if, after a time, administrators feel that this sector has received more than its fair share of available monies. The concept of 'fair shares' is a powerful one in DF allocation decisions. I shall return to it later.

From my observations, these three factors played a significant part in preparing the ground for the current emphasis being placed upon community health services. Change, then, is possible but only if a certain climate is created both within and without the NHS.

As well as being fluid and random, the allocation process is also messy. This is not caused by a lack of information *per se*, since information does exist to assist those responsible for allocating DF. Whether this information is assembled correctly or used to its best advantage are different matters. For example, staffing norms exist in nursing (the Aberdeen formula, approved by the SHHD), and various paramedical groups are moving in this direction too. There is a problem over the reliability of these norms. They do tend to veer towards the ideal rather than towards what might be acceptable. However, a more severe problem occurs if understaffing is present in several areas of nursing and all these gaps are listed as 'A' priorities—how does one decide whose requirements are the most urgent? For example, if a health board has a low level of nursing staff in a mental hospital and a low level of community nursing staff, the problem is to decide which has the higher priority. Faced with these dilemmas of choice, administrators cope in various ways.

For a start, many simply prefer a situation where funds are in short supply—then it is easy to say 'no' to everybody. If funds are reasonably plentiful, although still insufficient to satisfy all demands made upon them, then awkward decisions must be made—administrators dislike saying 'no' to some people and 'yes' to others.

As I said earlier, submissions for DF always far outstrip the funds available. Therefore, pruning and trimming become necessary so that the lists of requests for funds can be brought into line with the resources available. These are the principal weapons in the armoury of those administrators engaged in the allocation exercise. The reference to weapons is not far from the truth—the allocation exercise, according to one DA, can be quite bloody!

The development lists themselves can best be described as 'shopping-lists' of deficiencies—they are not linked to any specific policy objectives, or to any broad development strategy. The lists are made up from requests received direct from staff, from heads of departments, and from professional advisory committees. So, from the start, decision-makers are involved in a *reactive process* as opposed to an *anticipatory process*. Moreover, by asking staff about their wants, needs, shortages and pressure points (although most staff rather philosophically resign themselves to not having any of their demands met) the whole exercise merely serves to raise expectations which administrators then have to try and satisfy.

Having received these long lists of submissions, the officers (at Area and District) review them and concentrate on each submission in isolation, without relating it to any particular goals or objectives. Exceptions to this do occur but they remain exceptions. For example, perhaps a DA during an allocation meeting with other DOS might point out that a particular request for additional staff was in line with board policy on, say, geriatric care, or, conversely, that a request for a heart specialist would go against board policy if acceded to. But the overall tendency, especially at District level where detailed allocations occur, is to review each development in a vacuum. Decisions are taken in a somewhat piecemeal fashion. Although this approach prevents any examination of the total field, or problem area, and of alternative ways of allocating resources, it is simpler for a decision-maker to 'separate' problems in this way. At the same time, there exists an inertia, whereby it is easier to agree to new appointments rather than to look beyond the immediate need for additional staff in order to examine the form of care provided and possibly alter this. As I have already said, new staff appointment decisions are important because little-by-little they alter or, more usually, reinforce the pattern of care and the board is then committed to this pattern. And if the trend is to reinforce existing patterns of care through additional appointments, then altering the *status quo* becomes increasingly difficult. But administrators rarely look at a problem, or a request for more staff, with panoramic vision—they reduce a problem in size and consider only a limited number of options to resolve it.

It is not solely cognitive deficiencies or insufficient information which account for this approach to DF allocations. While there is certainly puzzlement about the objectives the NHS ought to be pursuing, there are also political reasons, in the form of vested interests and constant pressures arising from existing services, for operating at the margin but no further.

Changes may occur in this style of decision-making as a result of the publication of the SHHD's strategy memorandum, *The Way Ahead*, published in April 1976, and as a result of the outcome of the deliberations of the Scottish Health Service Planning Council's health priorities working party (see progress report, 1977). *The Way Ahead* does seem to have had some impact on health board operations. I only managed to observe initial reactions to the document. Board members were more enthusiastic about it than officers. Many of the latter claimed its usefulness was limited either because of its generality (i.e. it didn't take account of local gaps in services, including those the document recommended should not continue to grow), or because it did not add anything to what they already knew. Nevertheless, the document does seem to have provided some sort of yardstick or set of guidelines by which administrators and, more especially, board members can steer the services they provide.

In the absence so far of objectives or any overall strategy, decision-makers have to make some sense of their environment, and make some attempt to structure it in order to cope. They do this by devising their own tactics and strategies for allocating DF. These do not remove all conflicts but they do enable a decision-maker to reach decisions quite quickly within a framework which provides him with justifications for reaching a particular decision.

A major conflict which does remain despite this structuring concerns whether DF should be used to change the direction of services provided, or whether they should be used instead to plug gaps in existing services. If you do one, you can't do the other, and if you emphasise the latter then it becomes increasingly difficult to do the former because one is reinforcing existing services, and the vested interests associated with them which must be added to the annual clamour for more resources. This dilemma might be termed *policy stress*. In practice, the dilemma is easily resolved. DF tend to be used to eliminate deficiencies—'putting out fires'—since there is constant pressure from existing services for more resources (hence the phrase 'priorities by decibels'). The pressures to initiate a change of direction are not heard so loudly or clearly and usually come from outside the Service. Policy stress can also occur when there exist two current policies which are not strictly compatible with one another. For example, to shift the emphasis towards community care is not compatible with the appointment of more consultants if they establish more firmly the institutional orientation of the Service.

But despite these conflicts and dilemmas for which there is no rational, normative solution, although administrators may claim that they are acting rationally within the confines of the environment in which they operate, various tactics, or *aids to calculation*, are at the disposal of decision-makers to assist them in making their task slightly easier when allocating DF. I'd like to consider five of these which I observed in use (not all were explicit—some were implicit in the course of discussions over allocations):

(i) *Fair shares*. DF are often allocated on the basis of fair shares all round rather than on the basis of directing all available funds to one particular development. This has the effect of perpetuating the existing system of service provision which, correspondingly, lessens the chances of introducing any major innovations in the direction taken by particular services.

(ii) *Whom will it hurt least?* Who can do without an injection of funds—perhaps one of the ancillary services which has no direct impact on the treatment of patients.

(iii) *Who has done all right so far?* If some group did particularly well in a previous year, they will probably receive less in a subsequent year on the grounds that they have done well and that it is now someone else's turn.

(iv) *Who has had too much in relation to the rest?* If some group appears to have received a generous allocation at an early stage in the negotiations, some of this may be creamed off in order to ease pressures elsewhere.

(v) *Who has over/underspent?* If a head of expenditure is overspent, then it is unlikely to receive additional funds (with the possible exception of nursing which has historically been a special case in many health authorities prior to reorganisation) as a sanction against further overspending. If underspent, questions are likely to be asked concerning the suitability of further allocations if the possibility exists that they won't be spent during the financial year.

The general rule governing DF allocation decisions is that 'something is better than nothing'. A policy of appeasement is preferred, the aim being to keep as many people happy as possible. So DF are spread thinly over all the services provided within an area (occasionally a sudden crisis might upset this strategy, i.e. severe staff shortages which might lead to a public outcry if not remedied, and the entire DF allocation may be used to correct the situation). However, the overall tendency is to parcel out amounts to all the 'A' priorities and try to meet all these.

Administrators I have spoken to are ambivalent about the merits of this method of allocation. On the one hand they believe it to be unsatisfactory and that the only way to improve a service dramatically is to channel the whole of the available development monies into a particular area which is obviously underfinanced. There should be less and less of little bits of money being spent on a clerkess here, two nurses there, and an engineer somewhere. Yet, on the other hand, the same administrators argue, what *do* you do when faced with requests for DF for additional staff, which came in one smallish board to just under £1 million in the financial year 1975/76? There are so many understaffed areas and so many which should be strengthened. Consequently, there may well be something to be said for trying to improve a little bit here and there. As one Secretary explained, what do you do when a consultant's work-load increases beyond the point at which he can reasonably manage? Do you tell him to stop seeing patients as soon as he's doing more work than he should? You very quickly get caught up in a momentum. If patients appear, they must be seen. There may be other policy options which could usefully be explored but administrators are concerned predominantly with short-term considerations and the solutions they reach in response to particular pressures reflect this short-term thinking, or 'crisis management' approach to DF allocations.

This allocation strategy, whereby everyone receives something if at all possible, may be termed the *ratchet principle* (each group receives the same as last year only more if possible). Terms like *incrementalism* and *satisficing* can be used to describe the process. However even a term like incrementalism suggests a more ordered sequence of events than actually occurs. I would want to emphasise the *disjointedness* of the process. The allocation decisions I observed could be very messy and lacked continuity or consistency. When pruning and trimming become necessary, the operation develops into brutal horse-trading, resulting in crude trade-offs between staff establishments—for example, one radiographer might be agreed to if only two physiotherapists are recruited instead of the three originally requested, and so on.

In some instances, the allocation process may be simplified by the intervention of external factors beyond the control of decision-makers. For example, if seven health visitors are requested and it is impossible to recruit them because of a shortage of trained staff, then the decision is easy since it will have been pre-empted. However, the reverse of this situation can also occur. Scarce staff, like physiotherapists, can suddenly become available. Pressure is exerted on decision-makers to allocate funds to recruit them while they are available.

To sum up what I have been saying, existing allocations to services within health boards are not disturbed or reviewed—the battles for resources occur over DF since they represent the only free monies available for allocation. In the absence of an agreed approach to the problem of deciding priorities, the decisions made tend to reflect the current conventional wisdom about priorities generally within the NHS—these change when national fashions and public opinion begin to change (community care services illustrate this process). This is hardly surprising given the complexity of deciding priorities. Not much attention is given to the effectiveness of existing services (although administrators talk of having to do this now that the NHS is in a 'low-growth' situation). Questions of priority are primarily dealt with by deciding whether more, rather than less, of the current pattern of services should be provided in the future, or whether services should be maintained at current levels of provision (i.e. no change).

DF are needed in the majority of cases for 'first-aid' but sometimes they are committed by various projects already in existence, or about to come into existence, like ordinary capital schemes involving running-costs which must be met out of DF if the particular units are to come into operation. In the allocation process, pressure is also in the direction of bolstering up a service which is really unsatisfactory. There is no attempt to tackle a particular area of care and provide the resources which will, for example, allow geriatrics to be looked after as well as they might at home by keeping them out of hospital. Health boards do not appear to focus upon any major programme or area of care, like child health or care of the mentally ill. It comes down simply to a matter of fighting one's own corner to get resources in terms of inputs, i.e. additional numbers of staff. I'm not saying this system is wrong. Nor is the scenario I have just put before you necessarily going to remain unchanged. With the existence of health board programme planning groups currently investigating certain areas of health care, the whole approach to DF allocations outlined above may change as a result of the introduction of a new set of pressures and demands for resources.

However, in view of the constraints operating and the coping strategies decision-makers adopt to manage the uncertainties of their environment, it may be that the processes I observed are 'rational' in the sense that they are realistic and take account of the *political* nature of the environment where a number of professional groups jostle for a 'slice of the cake'. Any other approach might be totally unrealistic and impracticable and, therefore, unworkable.

(b) *The New Management Structure*
The case study has provided some insights into the management structure which has emerged from the reorganisation of the NHS. Most interestingly, the study reveals a number of *tension points*. These tensions can be grouped under two broad categories: (1) aims of reorganisation; (2) complexity of the management structure.

Two of the principal aims of reorganisation are:
(i) to improve efficiency and effectiveness through a better use of resources which, in turn, depends on improved management;
(ii) to allow for a greater measure of participation by the providers and consumers of health care in the decision-making process.

The question one wants to pose in relation to these twin objectives is, are they compatible, or does the achievement of one depend on the necessary failure, or distortion, of the other? Much of the tension I sensed, and the large number of criticisms of, and frustrations with, the new structure, stemmed from this dilemma and the inherent conflict to which it gives rise. Even in DF allocation decisions, the need to consult widely was a constraint on the ability of health boards to take speedy decisions.

Under (2) above, I would list the following tension points:

(i) the changed role of board members and officers and the relationship between them;

(ii) a closer relationship between area Officers and District Officers (resulting from the line management structure) than that which operated between the old RHBs and BOMs;

(iii) the possibility of role conflict inherent in the dual role of district Officers: for example, in a particular situation, should they remain loyal to the DEG of which they are members, or to their Area counterparts to whom they are directly accountable?

(iv) the problem of maintaining a clear distinction between those issues an officer refers to his executive group, and those decisions he should take himself within his own responsibilities;

(v) a feeling that sector administration (below the District level) has been neglected and was created more as an afterthought than as an integral part of the management arrangements;

(vi) a pull towards the centre in each health board because of the hierarchical structure of the organisation, which can be a source of tension for those at lower management levels. Having Districts, or at least a two-tier structure (four tiers if the SHHD and sectors are included), have made conflict a clear possibility, whereas in a simpler structure, or one in which *collateral* (i.e. 'sideways' relationship) rather than *superior-subordinate* relationships prevailed, there might have been less opportunity for conflict to occur.

In the resource-allocation decisions I observed, all these tensions were apparent at some point to some degree. It is not possible here to comment on all of them but I should like to say something about the role of board members and how this has changed—it is one of the more significant outcomes of reorganisation and resembles changes which have also taken place in local government in recent years.

Since NHS reorganisation, and as a result of it, the role of board members has been confined to dealing with 'major policy and strategic planning decisions', while the officers have had delegated to them a wide range of powers to make a number of decisions without having to refer them to the board for approval, as well as implementing those decisions which must be referred to the board. Even the strategic policy-making role reserved for board members is influenced to a large extent by the kinds of information supplied by officers. If board members want to play a more involved role in decision-making, which they were in a position to do before reorganisation, this is no longer possible. Indeed, it is physically impossible for the small number of health boards (fifteen) to take, or explicitly to confirm, the same number of decisions as their predecessors did. The fifteen boards replace the 150 or so bodies previously responsible for the NHS in Scotland. Moreover, the number of lay people participating in NHS administration in Scotland has been reduced from over 1500 before 1974 to 276 since then. In addition, lay members are located in one authority as opposed to two under the previous structure. On any count, the points at which important decisions involving lay members are made as regards the local operation of the health service are drastically reduced.

The total effect of all these changes is that the role of board members and the impact they can make on decision-making has contracted considerably, despite an increase in the services for which they are responsible, while the role of officers has expanded. Board members are supposed, in theory, to act as individual managers, representing no particular local interest. Local Health Councils (LHCs) are now the representatives of the consumer. This new role of board members is most unclear (further confused by the publication of the SHHD document in 1974, *The NHS and the Community in Scotland*), and the majority of them *do* see themselves as representatives. This brings them into direct conflict with the role of LHCs and many board members resent the existence of these bodies. They think LHCs are duplicating their role as board members and, as a result, are rendering them superfluous. A number of board members revealed in conversation how uncertain they were of their role. Those members with experience of the previous structure were particularly unhappy. But overall there was a feeling of a lack of involvement in board decision-making. Attempts have been made to overcome this sense of detachment by arranging visits to hospitals, clinics and so on, but these are unable by their very nature fully to compensate for a general feeling of impotence and they can lead to board members becoming over-involved in detail and matters of day-to-day management which are not supposed to concern them.

DF allocations illustrate the changes I have described. The

extensive scale of delegation by the board to the chief officers includes authority to vary staffing establishments and create new posts. The responsibility is on members of the AEG or DEG, not as before to present a case to the board in their individual capacities and await the board's decision, but to agree among themselves what is the right decision to take and present this to the board for its approval.

The management style which is a significant feature of reorganisation has led to the creation of a system in which officers carrying major responsibilities are supervised by boards, instead of a system in which the concept is of boards assisted by officers. The new arrangement is a reversal of roles for board members and officers.

There is much more that could be said about the management arrangements but I hope I have conveyed some of the atmosphere of the environment I have been observing. I hope also that I have not given the impression that life in a health board is all conflict and tension. It is not. On the whole, officers interact well and interpersonal relationships appear to be quite close. Many executive groups are made up of officers who knew each other before reorganisation. Nevertheless, the tensions underlying the good humour, which largely stem from the politico-administrative problems within the NHS rather than from personality clashes, do have a strong bearing on the decision-making process and can affect the flow of information, the use made of it, and the relationships which exist between different tiers.

To end on a note of caution, I must emphasise that my observations stem from only two health boards. It is never wise to generalise from one case study. Other boards may operate quite differently (admittedly unlikely) and allocate their DF using other tactics and strategies (again, unlikely). This paper has highlighted what appear to be some of the trends, and explanations for particular actions, that are emerging from the case study and subsequent analysis of data. Its contents should be treated in this light.

Theoretical Note. I have located my paper against a background which assumes the existence of a rational model of decision-making in the NHS. Indeed, this assumption is implicit throughout the paper, particularly where I discuss what might be termed deviations from rationality, or the 'limited rationality' thesis.

I have not plucked this rational model out of thin air. It seems to me that the reorganisation of the NHS in 1974 was concerned, to a very large extent, with improving decision-making by streamlining the administrative structure which would allow decision-making to become more efficient, more effective and more rational. It has always been clear that reorganisation was largely about management and how this might be improved. Ideas and concepts were borrowed from industry in the private sector and in England, the DHSS commissioned a team of management consultants from McKinsey & Co and a team from Brunel University to draw up the management arrangements for the reorganised Service. Although Scotland did not move so vigorously in a managerial direction, there was an overspill of the 'managerial style' from the English Grey Book (1972) into the Scottish Health Service reorganisation. Moreover, the Farquharson-Lang report (1966), which foreshadowed much of the management philosophy of the early 1970s, had some influence on the SHHD's thinking. Concepts like the separation of community representation from the management of health services, a key feature of the new structure, comprise this managerial style.

By rationality I am referring to a range of techniques and processes which have been advocated as being essential in any resource-allocation decision process. A rational model of decision-making comprises a number of explicit decision stages: (a) identification of a problem; (b) consideration of all the alternatives available; (c) identification and evaluation of all the consequences which would follow from the adoption of each alternative; (d) selection of that alternative which is optimal in relation to the desired objective. A rational model also involves the use of particular techniques, like operational research, management accounting, position statements and output budgets, to enable rational decisions to be made.

In the reorganised NHS, the uplifted role of the Treasurer is significant since he is entrusted with the task of introducing and applying many of these techniques. In the case of the medical profession, Community Medicine Specialists are also expected to inject some rationality into decisions taken by doctors at the sharp end of the Service.

Most important, a rational model of decision-making pre-supposes the existence of a consensus within an organisation, among those involved in taking decisions. The higher the rationality in a decision process, the greater emphasis is placed upon consensus and a corporate approach to decision-making and upon 'technical' criteria for the evaluation of expenditure proposals; the lower the rationality, the greater the emphasis is upon political 'wheeling and dealing' and incrementalism.

My paper has attempted to show how in practice, in the setting of a particular decision process (allocation of development funds), rationality is limited by the organisational and political environment which exists at health board level.

In particular, I have emphasised the importance of the budgetary process as an integral part of the political system which exists within any organisation. In this case, the budget is concerned with who gets what the health board has to give. The present circumstances of a diminished economic base have sharpened the choices that have to be made between competing claims. My research is an attempt to describe, or to 'map', part of this process.

From my observations, I have put forward the theory of incremental decision-making as an explanation of the decision process I examined. Much of incremental theory is concerned with the severely limited capacity of individuals to comprehend the full complexities of organisational and budgetary life. The decision-maker has to simplify reality because a comprehensive examination of it is intellectually impossible. There is much truth in this account of incrementalism but it does not fully explain limited rationality. The implication is that incrementalism could be avoided, or reduced, if better information were available. In an account of incrementalism as important, and possibly more important, is the view that budgets, or resource-allocations, are the outcome of clashes between entrenched interests (the clashes need not always actually occur; anticipation of them may be sufficient for decision-makers to attempt to avoid or minimise them).

What I am stressing is not merely the cognitive deficiencies of decision factors, but the political features of organisational life (see Greenwood *et al.*, 1977). An explanation of incrementalism must capture the bargaining, the negotiating and political nature of organisational phenomena and the conflicts of groups within the organisation. The way in which a health board is run, its organisational arrangements and procedures, directly affects the decision process surrounding resource-allocations.

This account of incrementalism helps to explain why some decisions are more, or less, incremental than others. The example cited in the paper where an attempt was made to alter the *status quo* in a somewhat less incremental fashion is community care. The focus on community care was the outcome of a political dialogue at local and national levels, particularly the latter. It was not the outcome of some rational analysis.

151

Appendix 2

REFERENCES

Brown, R. G. S. *et al. New Bottles: Old Wine?*, 4th report, Humberside
  Reorganisation Project, Institute for Health Studies, University of Hull,
  September 1975.

Chapman, R. (1968) *Decision Making*. London: Routledge & Kegan Paul.

Dearlove, J. (1973) *The Politics of Policy in Local Government*. Cambridge.

DHSS (1972) *Management Arrangements for the Reorganised NHS*. London:
  HMSO.

DHSS (1976) *Sharing Resources for Health in England*, report of the Resource
  Allocation Working Party. London: HMSO.

Friend, J. K. and Jessop, W. N. (1969) *Local Government and Strategic Choice*.
  London: Tavistock.

Friend, J. K. *et al.* (1974) *Public Planning: the intercorporate dimension*.
  London: Tavistock.

Greenwood, R. *et al.* (1977) 'The Politics of the Budgetary Process in English
  Local Government', *Political Studies*, 25, pp. 25-47.

Heclo, H. and Wildavsky, A. (1974) *The Private Government of Public Money*.
  London: Macmillan.

Heclo, H. (1975) 'Social Politics and Policy Impacts' in Holden, M., Jr. and
  Dresang, D. L. eds., *What Government Does*, pp. 151-76. Beverley Hills:
  Sage.

Institute for Operational Research. *Programme of Studies in Health Planning
  April 1974 – May 1976*, IOR/883R, Edinburgh, May 1976.

Klein, R. (1974a) 'Policy-Making in the NHS', *Political Studies*, 22, March,
  pp. 1-14.

Klein, R. (1974b) 'Policy problems and policy perceptions in the NHS',
  Policy and Politics, 2, No. 3, pp. 219-36.

Klein, R. ed. (1975) *Social Policy and Public Expenditure 1975: Inflation and
  Priorities*. Centre for Studies in Social Policy/Macmillan, London.

Kogan, M. (1975) *Educational Policy-Making*. London: Allen and Unwin.

Kogan, M. (1976) Book Review, *Political Quarterly*, 47, No. 4, pp. 490-1.

Layfield Committee (1976) *Local Government Finance*: report of the
  Committee of Inquiry, Appendix 6: 'The Relationship between Central
  and Local Government'. Commissioned work by R. A. W. Rhodes.
  London: HMSO.

Parry, G. and Morriss, P. (1974) 'When is a Decision not a Decision?' in
  Crewe, I., ed., *British Political Sociology Yearbook*, volume 1, pp. 317-36.
  London: Croom Helm.

Ridley, F. F. (1972) 'Public Administration: Cause for Discontent', *Public
  Administration*, 50, Spring, pp. 65-77.

Scottish Health Service Planning Council (1977) *Progress Report*, Working
  Party on Health Priorities, Edinburgh, unpublished.

SHHD (1966) *Administrative Practice of Hospital Boards in Scotland*,
  Farquharson-Lang Committee. Edinburgh: HMSO.

SHHD (1974) *The NHS and the Community in Scotland*. Edinburgh: HMSO.

SHHD (1976) *The Health Service in Scotland: The Way Ahead*. Edinburgh:
  HMSO.

SHHD (1977) *Scottish Health Authorities Revenue Equalisation*: report of the
  Working Party on Revenue Resource Allocation. Edinburgh: HMSO.

Schon, D. (1971) *Beyond the Stable State*. London: Temple Smith.

Taylor, R. (1977) 'The Local Health System: an Ethnography of Interest-
  Groups and Decision-Making'. *Social Science and Medicine* II, pp. 583-92

Wildavsky, A. (1964) *The Politics of the Budgetary Process*. Boston: Little,
  Brown.